GRAMMAR

BEAN

그

지은이	NE능률 영어교육연구소
선임연구원	김지현
연구원	이지영 차연경
영문 교열	Nathaniel Galletta August Niederhaus
디자인	박정진 오솔길 김명진
내지 일러스트	정경호
내지 사진	www.shutterstock.com
맥편집	김선희

GRAMMAR BEAN 2

정답 및 해설

UNIT 01 현재진행형

A 나는 매일 영어를 공부해요.
→ 나는 지금 영어를 공부하고 있어요.
그 아이들은 밤늦게 잠자리에 들어요.
→ 그 아이들은 지금 잠자리에 드는 중이에요.

C 우리는 지금 호텔에 머물고 있어요.
→ 우리는 지금 호텔에 머물고 있지 않아요.
Tiffany는 음악을 듣고 있어요.
→ Tiffany는 음악을 듣고 있지 않아요.

D 당신은 쿠키를 먹고 있어요.
→ 당신은 쿠키를 먹고 있나요?
- 네, 그래요. / 아니요, 그렇지 않아요.
그는 산책하고 있어요.
→ 그는 산책하고 있나요?
- 네, 그래요. / 아니요, 그렇지 않아요.

My Grammar Notes p.9

1. is running 2. not, not reading
3. 주어, Are they

Step1 Warm-Up p.10-11

A 1, 3, 5, 6, 7, 8

B 1. brushing 2. walking 3. study
4. flying 5. smiles 6. eating
7. skates 8. making

C 1. is∨riding 2. am∨doing
3. are∨running 4. is∨cleaning
5. are∨singing 6. is∨playing
7. is∨talking 8. are∨sitting

D 1. swimming 2. crying 3. going 4. Is
5. I 6. he teaching 7. they jumping
8. looking

Step2 Practice p.12-15

A 1. acting 2. crying 3. living
4. becoming 5. beginning
6. breaking 7. building 8. saying
9. stopping 10. dying 11. sitting
12. enjoying 13. lying 14. cutting
15. putting 16. coming

B 1. is buying 2. is waiting
3. are reading 4. is catching
5. am writing 6. is dancing
7. is running 8. are having

C 1. is, isn't driving
2. am, am not using
3. are, aren't[are not] listening
4. is, isn't[is not] snowing
5. are, aren't[are not] wearing

D 1. are, Are you 2. is, Is Mom
3. are, Are the boys
4. are, Are they 5. is, Is he

E 1. isn't looking
2. aren't[are not] singing
3. am not cooking
4. isn't[is not] barking
5. aren't[are not] riding
6. isn't[is not] wearing
7. aren't[are not] playing

F 1. Are they watching 2. Is it raining
3. Is he listening 4. Are they eating
5. Is she standing 6. Are you reading
7. Is she using

G 1. are eating 2. is calling 3. is looking
4. aren't[are not] staying

5. Are you doing 6. Is 7. is jogging
8. isn't[is not] watching 9. telling
10. Are 11. are not[aren't]

Step3 Grammar into Writing p.16-17

A
1. The girl is wearing yellow rain boots.
2. He isn't[is not] reading the newspaper.
3. Are they speaking in English?
4. Is Alex making chicken curry?
5. My friends are waiting for the bus.

B
1. 1) am learning
 2) My sister is learning Chinese.
2. 1) are swimming
 2) They are lying in the park.
3. 1) Is, listening
 2) Is Chris playing a computer game?
4. 1) isn't playing
 2) Ted isn't[is not] watching TV.
5. 1) are eating
 2) We are drinking apple juice.

C

There are some children in a park. Tom and Mina is playing badminton. Mike is fling a kite. Greg is rideing a bike. Jessica does going down the slide.

↓

There are some children in a park. Tom and Mina are playing badminton. Mike is flying a kite. Greg is riding a bike. Jessica is going down the slide.

Wrap-Up Test p.18-20

1. ④ **2.** ① **3.** ② **4.** ④ **5.** ② **6.** are
7. ③ **8.** ④ **9.** ⑤ **10.** ② **11.** ⑤
12. they aren't
13. We are not waiting for a bus.
14. is not studying, is resting
15. Is, swimming, she isn't, is riding

1. 모음 1개와 자음 1개로 끝나는 동사는 마지막 자음을 한 번 더 쓰고 ing를 붙인다.
④ stoping → stopping
2. ① be동사 다음에는 동사원형이 바로 올 수 없다.
3. 현재진행형의 부정문: 주어+be동사+not+동사원형-ing
4. 현재진행형: 주어+be동사+동사원형-ing
5. 현재진행형의 의문문: be동사+주어+동사원형-ing?
6. 현재진행형과 현재진행형의 부정문은 '주어+be동사+(not+)동사원형-ing' 형태이고, be동사는 주어가 복수일 때 are을 쓴다.
7. 현재진행형: 주어+be동사+동사원형-ing
현재진행형의 의문문: be동사+주어+동사원형-ing? (자음+e로 끝나는 동사는 e를 삭제하고 ing를 붙인다.)
8. ④ eating → is eating 또는 eats
9. ① cutting → am cutting 또는 cut
② are jump → are jumping 또는 jump
③ is talks → is talking 또는 talks
④ don't running → aren't running 또는 don't run
10. ② be동사를 이용한 질문에는 be동사를 이용해 답한다.
11. ①②③④ is[Is], ⑤ are
12. 주어(your friends)가 3인칭 복수이므로 they를 쓰고, 부정의 대답이므로 are not의 줄임말인 aren't를 쓴다.

13. 현재진행형의 부정문: 주어+be동사+not+동사원형-ing

14. 현재진행형: 주어+be동사+동사원형-ing
현재진행형의 부정문: 주어+be동사+not+동사원형-ing

15. 현재진행형의 의문문: be동사+주어+동사원형-ing?

UNIT 02 be동사의 과거형

A 나는 지금 키가 커요. 나는 전에는 작았어요.
이번 주는 따뜻해요. 지난주는 추웠어요.

B 작년에 큰 축제가 있었어요.
지하철에 많은 사람들이 있었어요.

C Reo는 내게 친절했어요.
→ Reo는 내게 친절하지 않았어요.
그들은 유명한 가수들이었어요.
→ 그들은 유명한 가수들이 아니었어요.

D 그는 배우였어요.
→ 그는 배우였나요?
- 네, 그랬어요. / 아니요, 그렇지 않았어요.
당신들은 학교에 늦었어요.
→ 당신들은 학교에 늦었나요?
- 네, 그랬어요. / 아니요, 그렇지 않았어요.

My Grammar Notes p.23

1. was, were, was 2. weren't
3. 주어, Was, wasn't

Step1 Warm-Up p.24-25

A 1, 4, 5, 6, 7

B 1. was 2. was 3. were 4. were
5. was 6. were 7. was 8. were

C 1. was∨easy 2. was∨absent 3. was∨cold
4. was∨angry 5. were∨at 6. was∨any
7. were∨my 8. was∨good

D 1. Was she 2. Was I 3. Were they
4. Was the movie 5. Were the books
6. Were there 7. Was he
8. Were we

Step2 Practice p.26-29

A 1. is, He was 2. are, You were
3. are, They were 4. am, I was
5. are, We were 6. is, It was
7. is, She was

B 1. is, was 2. is, was 3. am, was
4. are, were 5. are, were 6. were, are
7. was, is

C 1. There was 2. There are
3. There were 4. There was
5. There is 6. There were
7. There were

D 1. is 2. was 3. is 4. were 5. are
6. was 7. were

E 1. was, wasn't polite
2. were, weren't[were not] noisy
3. was, wasn't[was not] a smart boy
4. were, weren't[were not] big
5. was, wasn't[was not] a bad choice
6. was, wasn't[was not] great
7. was, wasn't[was not] surprised

F 1. Was the room, it wasn't
2. Were they, they were
3. Was the dress, it was
4. Was he, he wasn't

5. Was she, she was

6. Were the snacks, they weren't

G 1. were 2. was 3. Was

4. weren't[were not] 5. Was

6. wasn't[was not] 7. were 8. was

9. was 10. wasn't[was not] 11. Were

Step3 Grammar into Writing p.30-31

A 1. The wind was very cold.

2. His hands were warm.

3. The key was not[wasn't] under the table.

4. Were you at the library?

5. Was the weather good?

B 1. 1) was 2) We were sad yesterday.

2. 1) wasn't 2) The people weren't[were not] sleepy.

3. 1) were 2) There was a clock in the classroom.

4. 1) was 2) My parents were in Seoul last week.

5. 1) Were 2) Was your computer broken that day?

C Jina and I are good friends, but we are very different. Jina is short, but I am tall. Jina is good at math, but I'm not. There was a math test in school yesterday. It was very easy for Jina. Was it easy for me? No, it wasn't!

↓

지나와 나는 좋은 친구이지만, 우리는 매우 달라요. 지나는 키가 작지만, 나는 키가 커요. 지나는 수학을 잘하지만, 나는 그렇지 않아요. 어제 학교에서 수학 시험이 있었어요. 그것은 지나에게 매우 쉬웠어요. 그것이 나에게는 쉬웠을까요? 아니요, 그렇지 않았어요!

Wrap-Up Test p.32-34

1. ② **2.** ② **3.** ③ **4.** ② **5.** ③

6. it wasn't **7.** ③ **8.** ② **9.** ② **10.** ⑤

11. ③ **12.** ④ **13.** are → were

14. There was not a pond

15. Were, weren't

1. ② you – were

2. be동사 과거형의 부정문: 주어+was[were]+not ~.

3. ③ 주어가 3인칭 단수일 때 be동사의 현재형으로는 is나 isn't를, 과거형으로는 was나 wasn't를 쓴다.

4. ② 과거를 나타내는 문장이므로 now를 쓸 수 없다.

5. 과거를 나타내는 문장이고 주어가 I이므로 wasn't가 적절하다.

6. 주어가 3인칭 단수인 be동사의 과거 의문문에 대한 부정의 대답은 'No, 주어+wasn't.'가 적절하다.

7. 첫 번째 문장은 과거시제, 두 번째 문장은 현재시제이다.

8. ② 주어가 3인칭 단수인 be동사의 과거 의문문에 대한 긍정의 대답은 'Yes, 주어+was.'이다.

9. 주어가 3인칭 단수인 과거를 나타내는 문장이다.

10. ①②③④ was[Was], ⑤ were

11. ③ were → was

12. ④ 주어(they)가 복수이므로 were를 써서 답한다.

13. 과거를 나타내는 문장이고 주어가 복수이므로 were을 쓴다.

14. There+be동사의 과거형+not ~: ~가 없었다

15. 주어가 복수인 과거시제의 문장이므로 be동사 were를 이용한다. 앞에 Yes가 있지만 뒤에 light(가벼운)가 쓰였으므로 정황상 were의 부정형이 적절하다.

UNIT 03 일반동사의 과거형

My Grammar Notes p.37

1. 과거형 **2.** wanted, lived, cried, stopped
3. did, came, read, gave

Step1 Warm-Up p.38-39

A 1, 3, 6, 7, 11, 12, 14, 15, 17

B looked, sat, told, cried, wanted, made, came, did

C **1.** went **2.** played **3.** took **4.** bought
5. hoped **6.** fought **7.** gave **8.** hurt
9. stopped **10.** smiled **11.** said
12. read **13.** had **14.** knew
15. danced **16.** talked **17.** ate
18. planned **19.** cut **20.** heard

Step2 Practice p.40-43

A **1.** watched **2.** enjoyed **3.** loved
4. visited **5.** stopped **6.** helped
7. failed **8.** tried **9.** worked **10.** hated
11. passed **12.** talked **13.** washed
14. jumped

B **1.** met **2.** gave **3.** sang **4.** ran
5. drove **6.** sat **7.** came **8.** drank
9. slept **10.** had **11.** swam **12.** wrote
13. found **14.** made **15.** lost
16. taught **17.** got **18.** put

C **1.** listen, listened **2.** ate, eat
3. go, went **4.** cleans, cleaned
5. sees, saw **6.** exercises, exercised
7. begins, began **8.** know, knew
9. played, play **10.** buys, bought

D **1.** called **2.** dropped **3.** danced
4. cried **5.** waited **6.** had
7. played **8.** came

E **1.** met **2.** knew **3.** drank **4.** traveled
5. spoke **6.** ate **7.** planted

F **1.** was, am **2.** goes, went
3. taught, teaches **4.** has, had
5. lived, live **6.** wakes, woke
7. wanted, wants **8.** read, reading
9. opens, opened **10.** plays, playing

Step3 Grammar into Writing p.44-45

A **1.** watched TV **2.** met Jessica
3. made cookies **4.** studied English
5. saw a movie **6.** wrote e-mails
7. went shopping

B **1.** 1) snows
2) It snowed a lot last month.
2. 1) drives
2) He drove us home last night.
3. 1) helps
2) We helped him last week.
4. 1) read
2) Jack read a book yesterday.
5. 1) takes
2) I took piano lessons two years ago.

C

I went to an amusement park with my little brother yesterday. We ride the roller coaster and the merry-go-round. We eat pizza and drink Coke. We have a great time!

↓

I went to an amusement park with my little brother yesterday. We rode the roller coaster and the merry-go-round. We ate pizza and drank Coke. We had a great time!

Wrap-Up Test

p.46-48

1. ② **2.** ④ **3.** ⑤ **4.** ③ **5.** ② **6.** ④
7. ① **8.** ④ **9.** ④ **10.** ⑤ **11.** ④
12. swimed → swam **13.** does → did
14. He helped his parents
15. (1) came – come (2) sang – sing
(3) got – get

1. ② drop - dropped
2. ④ sit - sat
3. 과거를 나타내는 부사구(in 2015)가 쓰였으므로 과거시제로 써야 한다.
4. but 앞 문장은 반복되는 습관을 나타내므로 현재시제, 뒷 문장은 어제의 일이므로 과거시제로 쓴다.
5. 과거를 나타내는 표현(before, last night)이 쓰였으므로 둘 다 동사의 과거형이 들어가야 한다.
6. in 2012와 a month ago로 보아 두 문장 모두 과거시제로 써야 한다. give의 과거형은 gave이다.
7. ① 동사(painted)가 과거형이므로 now는 들어갈 수 없다.
8. last week은 과거를 나타내는 시간의 부사구이므로 과거시제로 써야 한다.
④ fights → fought
9. buy의 과거형은 bought이다.
10. ⑤ win → won
11. ① rain → rained ② meeted → met
③ lives → lived ⑤ begined → began
12. swim의 과거형은 swam이다.
13. does의 과거형은 did이다.
14. help의 과거형은 helped이다.
15. was: be동사, came / sang / got: 일반동사

UNIT 04 일반동사 과거형의 부정문과 의문문

A 나는 밤늦게 TV를 봤어요.
그는 빨래를 했어요.
우리는 어제 학교에 갔어요.

B 당신은 그 영화를 즐겼어요.
– 네, 그랬어요. / 아니요, 그렇지 않았어요.
그는 소파에서 잤어요.
– 네, 그랬어요. / 아니요, 그렇지 않았어요.
Tom과 Jane은 작년에 결혼했어요.
– 네, 그랬어요. / 아니요, 그렇지 않았어요.

My Grammar Notes

p.51

1. did, not, didn't 2. Did, Did 3. did

Step1 Warm-Up

p.52-53

A 1. didn't 2. don't 3. didn't 4. doesn't
5. didn't

B 1. didn't call 2. didn't do 3. didn't tell
4. didn't rain 5. didn't keep
6. didn't watch

C 1. Did, go 2. Did, drink 3. Did, buy

4. Do, take 5. Does, do 6. Did, arrive

D 1. I did 2. it did 3. they didn't
4. she did 5. I[we] didn't 6. he didn't

Step2 Practice p.54-57

A 1. Did, take 2. Did, wash 3. Did, read
4. Did, drink 5. Did, sing

B 1. met, meet 2. played, play
3. had, have 4. fixed, fix
5. taught, teach

C 1. Sara didn't go, Did Sara go
2. He didn't want, Did he want
3. They didn't bring, Did they bring
4. We didn't invite, Did we invite
5. He didn't miss, Did he miss
6. The train didn't leave,
Did the train leave
7. The children didn't break,
Did the children break
8. You didn't wear, Did you wear

D 1. didn't, got 2. took 3. played
4. didn't, went 5. do, I did 6. read
7. Yes, did 8. No, went

E 1. didn't read 2. started, didn't end
3. didn't swim, swam
4. Did, eat, ate 5. Did, go, enjoyed

F 1. Did you go 2. pass 3. like
4. didn't have 5. ride 6. I didn't
7. he didn't

Step3 Grammar into Writing p.58-59

A 1. She didn't take a bus.
2. He didn't[did not] go to the museum yesterday.
3. Did Daniel fight with his friend?
4. Did you make a snowman?

B 1. 1) didn't go
2) I didn't go to school yesterday.
2. 1) Did, read
2) Did he read today's newspaper?
3. 1) didn't wash
2) My father didn't wash his car.
4. 1) Did, forget
2) Did she forget your birthday?
5. 1) didn't lock
2) They didn't lock the door.

C
A: I'm so tired. I don't sleep last night.
B: Did you played games all night?
A: No, I did. I don't play games now.
B: What did you do yesterday?
A: I see a horror movie. It was very scary.

↓

A: I'm so tired. I didn't sleep last night.
B: Did you play games all night?
A: No, I didn't. I don't play games now.
B: What did you do yesterday?
A: I saw a horror movie. It was very scary.

Wrap-Up Test
p.60-62

1. ② 2. ③ 3. ④ 4. ④ 5. ③ 6. ③
7. ④ 8. did 9. ⑤ 10. ③ 11. ⑤
12. Did you meet
13. did not[didn't] wash her hair
14. Did the girls take the bus an hour ago?
15. (1) Yes, he did (2) No, he didn't

1. ② 일반동사 과거형의 부정문: 주어+didn't+동사원형
2. ③ 일반동사 과거형의 의문문: Did+주어+동사원형 ~?
3. 질문에 과거를 나타내는 시간의 부사구(a few days ago)가 쓰였으므로 과거시제를 써서 묻고 답해야 한다.
4. 그가 집에 머물렀다는 말이 이어지므로 정황상 부정의 대답이 알맞다.
5. 영화가 매우 재미있었다는 말이 이어지므로 정황상 긍정의 대답이 알맞다.
6. 일반동사 과거형의 부정문: 주어+didn't+동사원형
7. 일반동사 과거형의 의문문: Did+주어+동사원형 ~?
8. 일반동사 과거형의 부정문과 의문문은 주어에 상관없이 did를 이용하여 나타낸다.
9. didn't 뒤에는 동사원형을 써야 한다.
   ⑤ didn't made → didn't make
10. 일반동사 과거형의 의문문: Did+주어+동사원형 ~?
11. ① don't → didn't ② forgot → forget
    ③ didn't → doesn't ④ Does → Did
12. I didn't로 대답했으므로 you를 사용한 과거시제로 묻는 것이 자연스럽다. Ryan을 만났다는 대답이 이어지므로 질문에서는 동사원형 meet를 써야 한다.
13. 일반동사 과거형의 부정문: 주어+did not[didn't]+동사원형
14. 일반동사 과거형의 의문문: Did+주어+동사원형 ~?
15. (1) James는 늦게 일어나 지각했으므로 긍정의 대답인 'Yes, 주어+did.'를 써서 대답해야 한다.
    (2) James는 아침을 먹지 못했으므로 부정의 대답인 'No, 주어+didn't.'를 써서 대답해야 한다.

UNIT 05 형용사

B 1. 오래된 라디오 한 대
그는 부유한 사람이에요.
큰 나무들이 있어요.
그 더러운 양말들은 내 것이 아니에요.

2. 그의 귀여운 아기
나는 그녀의 갈색 눈을 좋아해요.
저것은 그들의 새 집이에요.
당신이 가장 좋아하는 가수는 누구인가요?

C 그들은 가난해요.
그녀는 친절해요.
하늘이 파래요.
그 집은 커요.

My Grammar Notes
p.65

1. 명사
2. bad, dirty, lazy, tall[long], old, poor
3. (1) 형용사, 명사 (2) be동사

Step1 Warm-Up
p.66-67

A lazy, fat, dry, young, handsome

B 1. ⓓ 2. ⓕ 3. ⓒ 4. ⓔ 5. ⓐ 6. ⓑ

C 1. There is a pretty flower.
2. This is my new computer.

3. Jenny has a big bag.
4. The singer has brown hair.
5. That is an old television.
6. Peter gives me sweet doughnuts.

D 1. delicious juice 2. tall boys
3. a small key 4. his white dog
5. a green apple 6. his blond hair
7. my new friends 8. her nice kitchen

E 1. ⓒ 2. ⓕ 3. ⓐ 4. ⓔ 5. ⓑ 6. ⓓ 7. ⓗ
8. ⓖ

Step2 Practice p.68-71

A 1. mine 2. love 3. have 4. my 5. are
6. place 7. a 8. room

B 1. This is my white shirt.
2. She is a kind teacher.
3. It is his old tablet.
4. He is an honest boy.
5. The blue bag is yours.
6. I love your sweet smile.
7. It's their new song.
8. The red skirt looks good.

C 1. tall, is tall 2. clean, are clean
3. happy, are happy 4. cold, am cold
5. expensive, is expensive
6. short, are short 7. fast, is fast
8. rich, is rich 9. small, is small
10. high, is high 11. new, is new

D 1. She is a smart student.
2. He has a brown rabbit.
3. Bob made a tasty sandwich.
4. There is a round table.
5. We visited a tall building.
6. It is a big balloon.
7. Sophia read interesting books.
8. Jennifer is a beautiful actress.
9. This is an old castle.
10. I have comfortable shoes.

E 1. is wise 2. is easy 3. is beautiful
4. is wonderful 5. was difficult
6. is empty 7. is hot 8. is exciting
9. were yellow

F 1. a kind boy 2. are cheap
3. Your black jacket 4. my pink socks
5. her lovely voice 6. Our new house
7. is cloudy 8. The old woman

Step3 Grammar into Writing p.72-73

A 1. This movie is boring.
2. My cats were fat.
3. The math question is difficult.
4. Her fingers are long.
5. That lake was deep.
6. Computer games are fun.

B 1. 1) green coat
2) Your green coat is warm.
2. 1) short boy
2) The short boy is smart.
3. 1) new laptop
2) My new laptop is expensive.
4. 1) old car
2) The old car is dirty.
5. 1) handsome prince
2) The handsome prince is lazy.

C

I am Cerberus. I have two heads. But I have three bodies. My faces and body are scary. My teeth are sharp. My body is yellow. My tail is short. My master is Hades. He is the god of death.

↓

I am Cerberus. I have three heads. But I have one body. My faces and body are scary. My teeth are sharp. My body is black. My tail is long. My master is Hades. He is the god of death.

Wrap-Up Test

p.74-76

1. ① **2.** ③ **3.** ④ **4.** ② **5.** ④ **6.** ③
7. ① **8.** are difficult **9.** ⑤ **10.** ③
11. ② **12.** ③ **13.** a diligent student
14. A hippo has a big mouth.
15. is a good sport

1. ① heart는 '심장, 마음'이라는 뜻의 명사이다.

2. ③ poor(가난한) – rich(부유한), kind(친절한) – unkind(불친절한)

3. 'a/an+형용사+명사'의 형태가 되어야 한다.

4. ② be동사 다음에는 명사나 형용사가 올 수 있다. like는 일반동사이다.

5. ④ 빈칸에는 뒤에 오는 명사(soccer player)를 꾸며주는 형용사가 들어가야 한다. world는 명사이다.

6. '주어+be동사+형용사'의 형태가 되어야 하고, '길다'의 의미를 갖는 형용사는 long이다.

7. 주어+be동사+형용사

8. 주어+be동사+형용사

9. ①②③④ 오래된, 낡은, ⑤ 나이가 많은

10. (a/an/the/소유격+) 형용사+명사
③ hair blue → blue hair

11. ① a pretty → pretty
③ Kind → The kind ('형용사+단수명사' 앞에 a, an, the가 필요하다.)
④ animals fast → fast animals
⑤ a small oranges → small oranges

12. '소유격+형용사+명사'의 형태가 되어야 하므로 my favorite singer가 알맞다.

13. 형용사(diligent)가 명사(student)를 꾸며주고, 'a/an+형용사+명사'의 형태로 쓴다.

14. 'a/an+형용사+명사'의 형태가 되어야 한다.

15. 'a/an+형용사+명사'의 형태로 쓴다. be동사(is)는 주어(swimming) 다음에 써서 '~이다'의 의미를 나타낸다.

UNIT 06 지시형용사, 수량형용사

B Mike는 많은 쿠키들을 만들고 있어요.
나는 많은 커피를 마시지 않아요.

C 꽃병에 꽃 몇 송이가 있어요.
꽃병에 꽃이 거의 없어요.
우리는 시간이 조금 있어요.
우리는 시간이 거의 없어요.

My Grammar Notes

p.79

1. that, these, those, 단수, these, those
2. many, much 3. few, a little

Step1 Warm-Up

p.80-81

A 1. This 2. This 3. That 4. That
5. Those 6. Those 7. These 8. These

B 1. this key 2. those toys 3. that library 4. this hot tea 5. these cupcakes 6. these oranges 7. that pretty garden 8. those cute rabbits

C 1. many 2. much 3. many 4. a lot of 5. a lot of 6. many 7. much 8. a lot of

D 1. a little 2. a few 3. few 4. a little 5. little 6. few 7. a few 8. a little

Step2 Practice

p.82-85

A 1. This 2. These 3. This 4. These 5. Those 6. That 7. Those 8. This

B 1. many 2. many 3. much 4. many 5. many, a lot of 6. much, a lot of 7. much, a lot of 8. many, a lot of

C 1. little 2. few 3. a little 4. little 5. a little 6. few 7. a few 8. few 9. a few 10. a few 11. few 12. few

D 1. This 2. That 3. These 4. Those 5. That 6. These 7. This 8. Those 9. That 10. This 11. Those

E 1. little sugar 2. a little money
3. many good friends
4. a few cute dogs
5. few trees 6. a little butter
7. much orange juice
8. a few old radios 9. little light
10. A few giant pandas

Step3 Grammar into Writing

p.86-87

A 1. These computers are brand-new.
2. I have a few backpacks.
3. I downloaded a lot of music.
4. There is little air in the rocket.
5. There are many books in the library.

B 1. 1) These
2) Those singers are famous.
2. 1) much[a lot of] 2) We don't have much[a lot of] rain in summer.
3. 1) many[a lot of] 2) She has many [a lot of] comic books.
4. 1) a few
2) There is a little sauce on the plate.
5. 1) little
2) There are few stars in the sky.

C

The witch visits Snow White's house. In the witch's basket, there are much apples. That apples look delicious. Snow White likes apples. But she has few money.

↓

The witch visits Snow White's house. In the witch's basket, there are <u>many[a lot of]</u> apples. <u>Those</u> apples look delicious. Snow White likes apples. But she has <u>little</u> money.

Wrap-Up Test

p.88-90

1. ⑤ **2.** ① **3.** ② **4.** ②, ③ **5.** ① **6.** ④
7. ③ **8.** ① **9.** ③ **10.** ⑤ **11.** ④
12. a little **13.** few **14.** This, These
15. There are a lot of horses

1. ⑤ a little은 '조금 있는'의 뜻이다.

2. ① 지시대명사(이것), ②③④⑤ 지시형용사(이 ~)

3. money는 셀 수 없는 명사이므로 앞에 much를

써야 한다.

4. 복수명사(fans) 앞에 쓸 수 있는 수량형용사는 many와 a lot of이다.

5. 단독(지시대명사)으로도 쓸 수 있고, 명사와 함께 쓸 수도 있는 것(지시형용사)은 This와 These이다. 빈칸에는 단수형이 적절하므로 This를 쓴다.

6. (a) few+복수명사 / (a) little+셀 수 없는 명사

7. a little+셀 수 없는 명사

8. ① These → This

9. time은 셀 수 없는 명사이므로 few가 아닌 little과 함께 쓰며, little(거의 없는)이 부정의 의미이므로 not을 쓸 필요가 없다.

10. ⑤ orange juice는 셀 수 없는 명사이므로 many가 아닌 much를 쓴다.

11. ④ a little → a few

12. help는 셀 수 없는 명사이므로 a little을 써서 '약간의, 조금의'라는 뜻을 나타낸다.

13. buses는 복수명사이므로 few를 써서 '거의 없는'이라는 뜻을 나타낸다.

14. roses가 복수이므로 These를 쓴다.

15. a lot of+복수명사

UNIT 07 who, what

B 누가 케이크를 더 원하나요?
당신은 누구를 가장 좋아하나요?
그것은 누구의 집인가요?

C 당신의 혈액형은 무엇인가요?
그는 어떤 일을 하나요?
지금이 몇 시인가요?
당신은 어떤 디저트를 좋아하나요?

My Grammar Notes p.93

1. who, when, what, how

2. (1) be동사 (2) 의문사, 동사원형

3. who, whom[who], whose **4.** what, 명사

Step1 Warm-Up p.94-95

A **1.** ⓑ **2.** ⓒ **3.** ⓐ **4.** ⓕ **5.** ⓔ **6.** ⓓ **7.** ⓖ

B **1.** is **2.** do **3.** is **4.** is **5.** does **6.** do **7.** was **8.** move **9.** did

C **1.** Whose **2.** Whose **3.** What **4.** What **5.** Who **6.** Who **7.** Whom **8.** Whom **9.** What **10.** What

D **1.** ⓒ **2.** ⓓ **3.** ⓐ **4.** ⓑ **5.** ⓖ **6.** ⓕ **7.** ⓔ

Step2 Practice p.96-99

A **1.** ⓑ **2.** ⓓ **3.** ⓒ **4.** ⓐ **5.** ⓔ

B **1.** are **2.** is **3.** do **4.** drives **5.** does **6.** do **7.** wants **8.** find **9.** visit **10.** meet

C **1.** What **2.** Whose **3.** Whom **4.** Who **5.** What **6.** Who **7.** What

D **1.** What **2.** What **3.** Who **4.** Whose **5.** Who[Whom] **6.** What

E **1.** Who **2.** like **3.** Whose **4.** Who[Whom] **5.** do **6.** Who **7.** meet **8.** is **9.** say

F **1.** Whose car is this?
2. What are you looking for?
3. Whose bicycle is it?
4. What did he give to her?
5. Who can solve the problem?
6. Who ate my ice cream?
7. What animal does she like?
8. Who is dancing on the stage?

G 1. Who 2. What 3. Who
4. Who[Whom] 5. Who 6. What
7. Whose 8. What 9. Whose 10. What
11. What 12. What 13. Who[Whom]
14. Who 15. What 16. Whose
17. What

Step3 Grammar into Writing

p.100-101

A 1. What is your favorite season?
2. Who won the match?
3. Whose shoes are these?
4. What subject do you hate?
5. What did they eat for lunch?

B 1. 1) Who 2) Who teaches Japanese?
2. 1) Whom[Who]
2) Whom[Who] did the actress marry?
3. 1) What 2) What color is her hair?
4. 1) Whose
2) Whose glasses are these?
5. 1) What
2) What do you wear on Halloween?

C whose, Who, What

Wrap-Up Test

p.102-104

1. ④ **2.** ④ **3.** ① **4.** ③ **5.** ① **6.** ⑤
7. ⑤ **8.** ② **9.** ④ **10.** ④ **11.** ⑤
12. What did you eat
13. Whom[Who] will he meet
14. Who broke the vase yesterday?
15. Whose book did you borrow at school?

1. ④ that은 지시대명사 또는 지시형용사이다.
2. 'What+명사'는 '무슨 ~, 어떤 ~'을 의미한다.
3. '누가'를 뜻하는 Who가 들어가야 한다.
4. '누구의 ~'를 뜻하는 Whose가 들어가야 한다.
5. ① Whose, ②③④⑤ What
6. ⑤ '누구를'의 의미로 쓰인 의문사는 Who 또는 Whom을 쓸 수 있다.
7. '치킨 버거를 가장 좋아한다'라는 대답이 나오려면 ⑤ '어떤 음식을 가장 좋아하니?'라고 묻는 것이 적절하다.
8. 누구인지 물을 때는 who를 쓰고, 무엇인지 물을 때는 what을 쓴다.
9. 의문사+did+주어+동사원형 ~?
④ What you did → What did you
10. ④ '누구의 ~'를 뜻하는 의문사는 whose이다.
11. ⑤ 누구를 봤는지 묻는 말에 영화를 봤다는 대답은 어색하다.
12. 대답으로 보아 무엇을 먹었는지 묻는 말이 적절하고, 과거시제로 대답했으므로 'What did+주어+동사원형'의 어순을 따른다.
13. 대답으로 보아 누구를 만날 것인지 묻는 말이 적절하고, 의문사 whom과 who 둘 다 쓸 수 있다.
14. '누가'라는 뜻의 주어 역할을 하는 의문사 who를 쓰고, 과거의 일을 묻고 있으므로 break의 과거형 broke를 써야 한다.
15. '누구의 ~'를 뜻하는 의문사 whose 뒤에는 명사가 와야 한다. 의문사 뒤에는 'did+주어+동사'의 어순을 취한다.

UNIT 08 where, when, why

B 당신은 어젯밤에 어디에 있었나요?
그들은 어디에 사나요?

C 그녀의 생일은 언제인가요?
첫 기차는 몇 시에 있나요?
그 뮤지컬은 언제[몇 시에] 시작하나요?

D 당신은 왜 기분이 좋은가요?
- 왜냐하면 시험에서 좋은 성적을 받아서요.
당신은 왜 저 가수를 좋아하나요?
- 왜냐하면 그는 노래도 매우 잘하고 춤도 매우 잘 추기 때문이에요.

My Grammar Notes p.107

1. where, when, why 2. where, Where
3. when, When, what time 4. why, because

Step1 Warm-Up p.108-109

A 1. are 2. is 3. steal 4. talk 5. get
6. is 7. does 8. did

B 1. X 2. X 3. O 4. O 5. O 6. X 7. X
8. O

C 1. ⓓ 2. ⓐ 3. ⓔ 4. ⓒ 5. ⓖ 6. ⓕ 7. ⓑ

D 1. Where 2. Where 3. Why 4. When
5. When 6. Why

Step2 Practice p.110-113

A 1. did 2. does 3. did 4. is 5. does
6. are 7. does 8. is

B 1. Where 2. When 3. When 4. Why
5. Why 6. Where 7. When 8. Why

C 1. Why 2. Where 3. When 4. Why
5. Where

D 1. ① 2. ② 3. ① 4. ② 5. ③

E 1. are 2. do 3. is
4. does the bus come 5. fight
6. did you 7. did you spend 8. send

F 1. When does the class begin?
2. Where did you play basketball?
3. Why do you look so happy?
4. What time does the show finish?
5. Why did you meet her yesterday?

G 1. Where are 2. Where is
3. Why do, exercise 4. When did, lose
5. Where did, put 6. What time did
7. Where did, happen 8. Why did, go
9. What time does, start 10. When is
11. When did, call

Step3 Grammar into Writing p.114-115

A 1. Where is Mark now?
2. Why is she laughing?
3. When do you get up in the morning?
4. What time does the musical start?
5. Where did you take this photo?

B 1. 1) Where 2) Where are my socks?
2. 1) What time
2) What time does he eat lunch?
3. 1) Why
2) Why does he like this soccer player?
4. 1) When
2) When did Sally buy this bag?
5. 1) Where
2) Where did James see Sophie?

C Why, When, Where

Wrap-Up Test p.116-118

1. ② **2.** ② **3.** ③ **4.** ④ **5.** ⑤ **6.** ④
7. ④ **8.** ③ **9.** ④ **10.** ① **11.** ②
12. Where did he find
13. What time does the train leave?
14. Why was she
15. When did you arrive at the airport?

1. ② where – 어디에
2. 시간을 나타내는 대답이 이어지므로 When이 적절하다.
3. 장소를 나타내는 대답이 이어지므로 Where가 적절하다.
4. 이유를 설명하는 대답이 이어지므로 Why가 적절하다.
5. 장소를 묻는 Where와 시간을 묻는 When이 각각 들어가야 한다.
6. ④ when은 시간을 묻는 의문사이므로, 시간을 나타내는 표현이 이어져야 한다.
7. ④ What time you → What time do you
8. 의문사가 있는 현재시제 의문문: 의문사+do[does]+주어+동사원형 ~?
9. Because를 사용하여 대답하므로 When 대신 Why를 써야 하고, 시간을 나타내는 표현(around 4 p.m.)을 사용하여 대답하므로 Why 대신 When 또는 What time을 써야 한다.
10. ① 감기에 걸린 이유를 묻는 질문에 열이 난다는 대답은 어색하다.
11. ⑤ 대답에서 이유를 나타내는 말은 없으므로, why로 물을 수 없다.
12. 의문사가 있는 과거시제 의문문: 의문사+did+주어+동사원형 ~?
13. 정확한 시각을 물을 때는 what time을 쓰고, 뒤에 'does+주어+동사원형 ~?'의 어순을 따른다.
14. Because를 사용하여 대답하므로 의문사 Why를 쓰고, '의문사+be동사+주어'의 어순을 따른다.
15. 의문사가 있는 과거시제 의문문: 의문사+did+주어+동사원형 ~?

UNIT 09 how

C 1. 교실 안에는 얼마나 많은 학생들이 있나요?
당신은 수프에 얼마나 많은 소금을 넣었나요?
2. 이 필통은 얼마인가요?
이 청바지는 얼마인가요?

My Grammar Notes p.121

1. how 2. (2) how tall (3) how often (4) how long 3. how many, how much 4. much

Step1 Warm-Up p.122-123

A 1, 2, 4, 6, 7

B 1. much 2. many 3. much 4. many 5. much 6. many 7. much 8. many

C 1. old 2. tall 3. long 4. often 5. much 6. many 7. much

D 1. ⓑ 2. ⓐ 3. ⓔ 4. ⓓ 5. ⓒ 6. ⓕ 7. ⓗ 8. ⓖ

Step2 Practice p.124-127

A 1. ⓔ 2. ⓕ 3. ⓐ 4. ⓑ 5. ⓓ 6. ⓒ

B 1. are 2. does 3. do 4. do 5. is 6. is 7. are 8. did

C 1. time 2. chairs 3. money 4. dog 5. pens 6. eggs

D 1. How many 2. How old 3. How often 4. How much 5. How long 6. How much

E 1. How old 2. How tall 3. How 4. How much 5. How long

6. How many 7. How 8. How much

9. How many 10. How often 11. How

F 1. How is 2. How often does

3. How much, does

4. How tall is 5. How long did

6. How did 7. How many, does

8. How old is 9. How much is

10. How many, did 11. How was

Step3 Grammar into Writing p.128-129

A 1. How much is this ring?

2. How tall is Seoul Tower?

3. How many cookies did you eat?

4. How often do you play soccer?

5. How did you make this cake?

B 1. 1) How much

2) How much milk did you drink?

2. 1) How often

2) How often does this subway run?

3. 1) How much

2) How much is this monitor?

4. 1) How long

2) How long is the Great Wall?

5. 1) How many

2) How many stars are there in the Milky Way?

C How do you, How often did you, How long[How many hours] did you

Wrap-Up Test p.130-132

1. ④ **2.** ④ **3.** ③ **4.** ① **5.** ④ **6.** ③

7. ③ **8.** ② **9.** ⑤ **10.** ③ **11.** ④

12. How often **13.** How much

14. How did you save

15. How many bananas are

1. ④ how many: 얼마나 많은

2. ④ peaches는 복수명사이므로 양을 묻는 how much 뒤에 쓸 수 없다.

3. ③ money는 셀 수 없는 명사이므로 수를 묻는 how many 뒤에 쓸 수 없다.

4. B의 대답으로 보아 시험이 어땠는지 묻는 말이 되어야 한다.

5. B의 대답으로 보아 얼마나 자주 전화하는지 묻는 말이 되어야 한다.

6. ③ how often을 이용해 횟수를 묻는 말에 적절한 대답이다.

7. ③ 뒤에 명사가 이어지고 의미상 Whose가 들어가는 것이 자연스럽다.

8. 첫 번째 빈칸에는 상태를 묻는 How가 적절하고, 두 번째 빈칸에는 셀 수 있는 명사가 이어지므로 수를 묻는 How many가 자연스럽다.

9. How many는 '얼마나 많은 ~'의 의미로 뒤에 셀 수 있는 명사가 와야 한다.
⑤ How many are bikes
→ How many bikes are

10. how tall: 얼마나 높은

11. ④ how much를 이용해 가격을 묻는 질문에 차를 한 대만 가지고 있다는 대답은 어색하다.

12. B의 대답으로 보아, '얼마나 자주'의 How often이 와야 함을 알 수 있다.

13. B의 대답으로 보아, 가격이 얼마인지 묻는 말이 와야 함을 알 수 있다.

14. How+did+주어+동사원형 ~?

15. banana는 셀 수 있는 명사이므로 how many를 쓰고, 'How many+명사+be동사'의 어순을 취한다.

UNIT 10 비인칭 주어 it

B 오후 7시예요.
5시 30분이에요.
10시 정각이에요.
4월 1일이에요.
7월 10일이에요.
8월 28일이에요.
월요일이에요.
일요일이에요.
토요일이에요.

C 화창해요. / 흐려요.
추워요. / 따뜻해요.
비가 내려요. / 눈이 와요.
봄이에요. / 여름이에요.
가을이에요. / 겨울이에요.

D 8마일이에요.
10킬로미터예요.
여기서부터 도서관까지는 5킬로미터예요.

My Grammar Notes p.135

1. it 2. It 3. day, it 4. It, rainy 5. is it

Step1 Warm-Up p.136-137

A 1. O 2. X 3. X 4. O 5. X 6. O 7. O
8. O

B 1. ⓑ 2. ⓔ 3. ⓓ 4. ⓒ 5. ⓔ 6. ⓒ 7. ⓐ
8. ⓕ

C 1. X 2. O 3. O 4. O 5. X 6. O 7. O
8. X 9. X 10. O

D 1. ⓐ 2. ⓔ 3. ⓑ 4. ⓒ 5. ⓕ 6. ⓓ

Step2 Practice p.138-141

A 1. It 2. It 3. This 4. It 5. It 6. There

B 1. ② 2. ① 3. ③ 4. ④ 5. ① 6. ②

C 1. ① 2. ① 3. ④ 4. ③ 5. ②

D 1. is it, It is 2. day, it 3. It is
4. far, it, It is

E 1. It, snow 2. What day, it
3. It was, warm 4. It is 5. What time, it
6. It is 7. It is, eight 8. It 9. It is far
10. It rained 11. It is 12. is it

F 1. It wasn't very windy yesterday
2. It is getting cold
3. How far is it from here
4. It is not Thursday
5. What is the date today
6. What season is it in Vietnam
[In Vietnam, what season is it]
7. It is hot in summer
[In summer, it is hot]
8. It is 11:20 now
9. What time is it now
10. It's far from here to the village
11. It is close to here
12. It's the second Sunday of January

Step3 Grammar into Writing p.142-143

A 1. ⓑ, 오늘은 12월 24일이야. 메리 크리스마스!
2. ⓖ, 밖이 무척 추워. 코트를 입으렴.
3. ⓒ, 금요일 밤이야. 영화 보러 가자.
4. ⓐ, 밤에 비가 올 거야. 우산을 가져와.
5. ⓔ, 여기서 시장은 멀어. 버스를 타.
6. ⓓ, 벌써 여름이야. 난 선풍기를 살래.
7. ⓕ, 지금 열두 시야. 점심을 먹자.

B **1.** It is hot **2.** What day is it
3. It is far **4.** It was **5.** It is summer
6. Is it

C **1.** It was warm and sunny.
2. it was far from our house
3. It was almost 8 p.m.

Wrap-Up Test

p.144-146

1. ③ **2.** ⑤ **3.** ② **4.** ③ **5.** ④ **6.** ②
7. How far is it **8.** ① **9.** ② **10.** ⑤
11. ④ **12.** ① **13.** It is ten ten.
14. It will be sunny and warm today.
15. What season is it?

1. ①②④⑤ 요일·날씨·시간·거리와 관련된 비인칭 주어 it, ③ 대명사 it

2. ①②③④ 시간·거리·계절·날짜와 관련된 비인칭 주어 it, ⑤ 대명사 it

3. 날짜(date)를 묻고 답하는 대화이다.

4. 날씨에 대해 묻고 있으므로, 비가 심하게 내리고 있다는 대답이 가장 알맞다.

5. 서점까지의 거리에 대해 묻고 있으므로, 집에서 멀다는 대답이 가장 알맞다.

6. 몇 시인지 묻고 있으므로, 7시 5분이라는 대답이 가장 알맞다.

7. B의 응답으로 보아 거리를 묻는 표현이 들어가야 한다.

8. ① 빈칸 뒤에 like가 있으므로 3인칭 단수 주어인 it은 들어갈 수 없다.

9. What's the weather like?
= How's the weather?

10. ①②③④ 각각 날짜·날씨·시간에 관련된 비인칭 주어, ⑤ a snowman을 가리키는 대명사

11. 거리를 나타낼 때는 비인칭 주어 it을 쓴다.
④ This → It

12. ① 계절을 묻는 말에 날씨에 대한 대답을 하는 것은 어색하다.

13. 비인칭 주어 it을 이용하여 시간을 표현한다.

14. 비인칭 주어 it을 이용하여 날씨를 표현한다.

15. 계절을 묻는 표현은 비인칭 주어 it을 이용하여 'What season is it?'으로 나타낸다.

MEMO

MEMO

MEMO

MEMO

MEMO

Beginning

Easy

Active

New

이제 시작이에요!
처음으로 문법을 공부하는 여러분, 두려워하지 마세요.
이제부터 Grammar Bean(그래머빈)이 영어에 대한
자신감을 가질 수 있게 도와줄게요.

구성과 특징

알기 쉬운 문법 설명

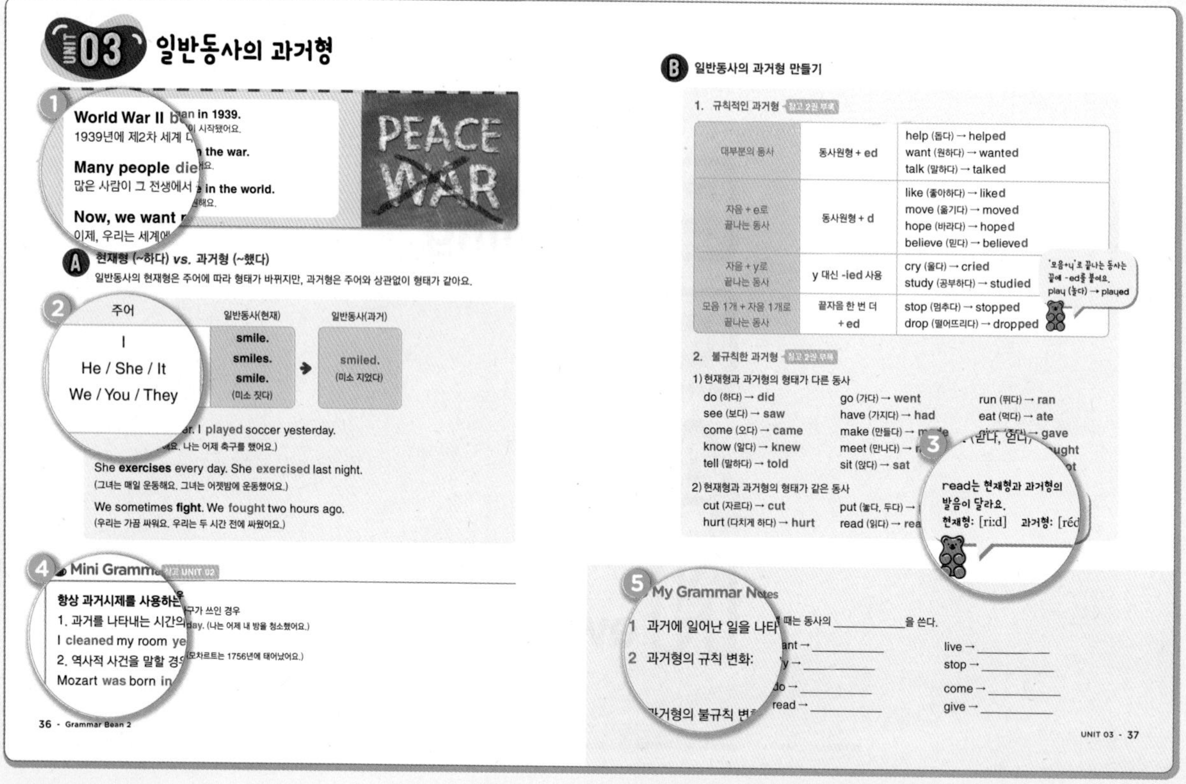
UNIT 03 일반동사의 과거형

World War II began in 1939.
1939년에 제2차 세계 대전이 시작됐어요.

Many people died in the war.
많은 사람이 그 전생에서 죽었어요.

Now, we want peace in the world.
이제, 우리는 세계에 평화를 원해요.

PEACE WAR

A 현재형 (~하다) vs. 과거형 (~했다)

일반동사의 현재형은 주어에 따라 형태가 바뀌지만, 과거형은 주어와 상관없이 형태가 같아요.

주어	일반동사(현재)	일반동사(과거)
I	smile.	smiled. (미소 지었다)
He / She / It	smiles.	
We / You / They	smile. (미소 짓다)	

I play soccer every year. I played soccer yesterday.
(... 나는 어제 축구를 했어요.)

She exercises every day. She exercised last night.
(그녀는 매일 운동해요. 그녀는 어젯밤에 운동했어요.)

We sometimes fight. We fought two hours ago.
(우리는 가끔 싸워요. 우리는 두 시간 전에 싸웠어요.)

Mini Grammar 참고 UNIT 02

항상 과거시제를 사용하는 경우
1. 과거를 나타내는 시간의 부사구가 쓰인 경우
I cleaned my room yesterday. (나는 어제 내 방을 청소했어요.)
2. 역사적 사건을 말할 경우
Mozart was born in 1756. (모차르트는 1756년에 태어났어요.)

36 · Grammar Bean 2

B 일반동사의 과거형 만들기

1. 규칙적인 과거형 참고 2권 부록

대부분의 동사	동사원형 + ed	help (돕다) → helped want (원하다) → wanted talk (말하다) → talked
자음 + e로 끝나는 동사	동사원형 + d	like (좋아하다) → liked move (옮기다) → moved hope (바라다) → hoped believe (믿다) → believed
자음 + y로 끝나는 동사	y 대신 -ied 사용	cry (울다) → cried study (공부하다) → studied
모음 1개 + 자음 1개로 끝나는 동사	끝자음 한 번 더 + ed	stop (멈추다) → stopped drop (떨어뜨리다) → dropped

'모음+y'로 끝나는 동사는 끝에 -ed를 붙여요.
play (놀다) → played

2. 불규칙한 과거형 참고 2권 부록

1) 현재형과 과거형의 형태가 다른 동사

do (하다) → did
see (보다) → saw
come (오다) → came
know (알다) → knew
tell (말하다) → told
go (가다) → went
have (가지다) → had
make (만들다) → made
meet (만나다) → met
sit (앉다) → sat
run (뛰다) → ran
eat (먹다) → ate
give (주다) → gave

2) 현재형과 과거형의 형태가 같은 동사

cut (자르다) → cut
hurt (다치게 하다) → hurt
put (놓다, 두다) → put
read (읽다) → read

read는 현재형과 과거형의 발음이 달라요.
현재형: [ri:d] 과거형: [réd]

My Grammar Notes

1 과거에 일어난 일을 나타낼 때는 동사의 ________을 쓴다.
2 과거형의 규칙 변화: want → ________ study → ________ live → ________ stop → ________
3 과거형의 불규칙 변화: do → ________ read → ________ come → ________ give → ________

UNIT 03 · 37

① 간단한 예문을 살펴보면서 학습할 내용을 예상해 보세요.

② 한눈에 들어오는 문법 정리와 예문으로 문법 내용을 쉽게 이해할 수 있어요.

③ 말풍선 안에는 주의해야 하거나 꼭 기억해야 할 내용이 있으니 꼼꼼히 챙겨 보세요.

④ Mini Grammar에서는 지금 공부하는 내용과 관련하여 추가적으로 알면 도움이 되는 문법 사항이 제시되어 있어요.

⑤ My Grammar Notes는 학습한 내용을 정리하는 코너예요. 빈칸을 채우면서 요점을 정리해 보세요.

다양한 유형의 3단계 Exercise + Test

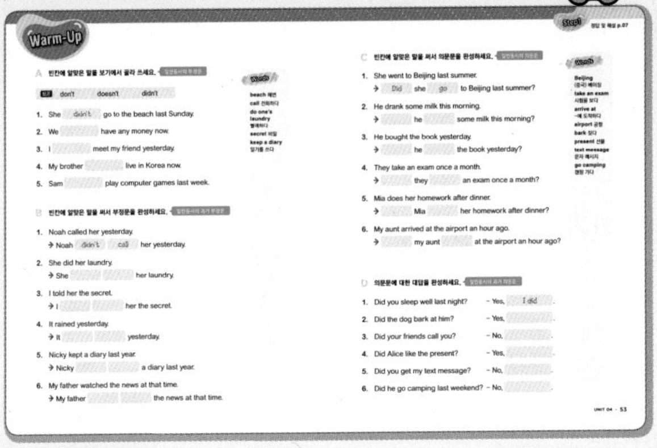

Warm-Up

새롭게 학습한 내용을 충분히 이해했나요? 간단한 문제를 통해 점검해 보세요.

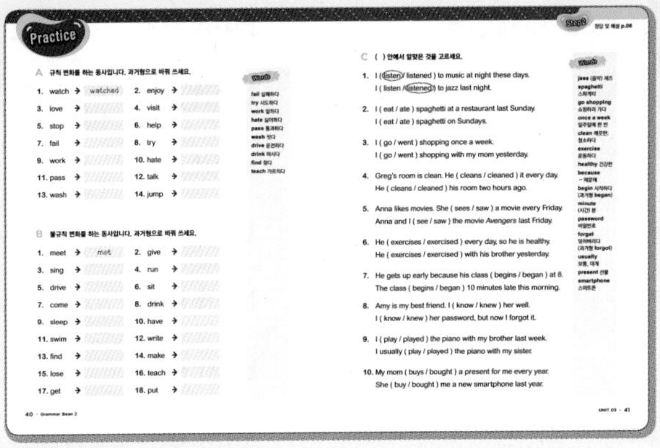

Practice

연습이 최선이라는 말 알고 있죠? 다양하고 많은 연습문제를 풀면서 자연스럽게 문법을 익힐 수 있어요.

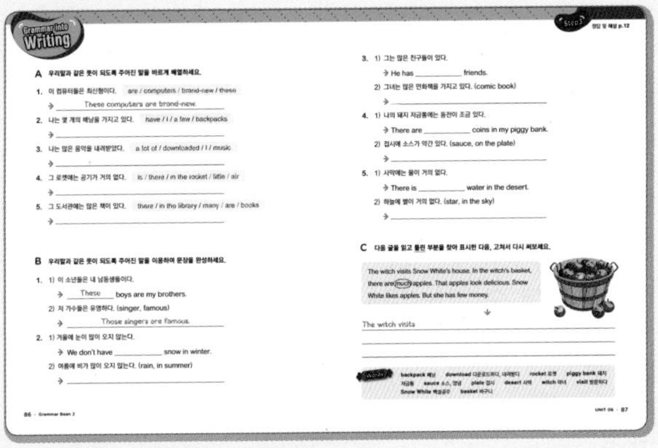

Grammar into Writing

문법을 배우는 목적이 문제 풀이와 시험만은 아니에요. 문법을 활용하면 영어 문장을 쓰는 것도 문제 없어요.

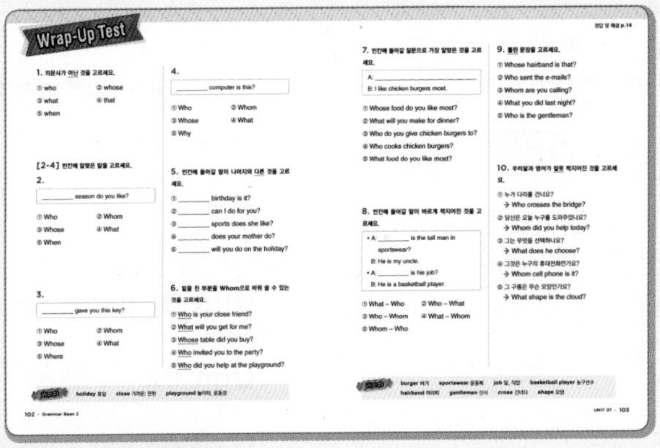

Wrap-Up Test

객관식 문제와 서술형 문제를 통해 배운 내용을 총정리해 보세요. 점수가 좋지 않으면 복습을 잊지 마세요.

+ Workbook

각 Unit별 연습문제와 별도의 Grammar Test가 수록되어 있어요.
Workbook을 통해 부족한 부분을 보충하고 배운 내용을 내 것으로 만들어 보세요.

CONTENTS

3권

4권

STUDY PLAN

차시	진도 현황 (교재)		숙제 (Workbook)	학습 날짜	복습 (O/X)	어휘 (전/후)
1차시	Unit 01	현재진행형		월 일		개 / 개
2차시				월 일		
3차시	Unit 02	be동사의 과거형		월 일		
4차시				월 일		
5차시	Unit 03	일반동사의 과거형		월 일		
6차시				월 일		
7차시	Unit 04	일반동사의 과거형의 부정문과 의문문		월 일		
8차시				월 일		
9차시	Unit 05	형용사		월 일		
10차시				월 일		
11차시	Unit 06	지시형용사, 수량형용사		월 일		
12차시				월 일		
13차시	Unit 07	who, what		월 일		
14차시				월 일		
15차시	Unit 08	where, when, why		월 일		
16차시				월 일		
17차시	Unit 09	how		월 일		
18차시				월 일		
19차시	Unit 10	비인칭 주어 it		월 일		
20차시				월 일		

❶ 숙제 칸에는 숙제 내용을 적고, 학습 날짜 칸에는 수업 날짜를 적어요.

❷ 오답 복습을 완료하면 복습 칸에 동그라미(O) 표시를 해요.

❸ 학습하기 전 모르는 어휘 개수를 칸 왼쪽에 적고, 학습 후 틀린 어휘 개수를 칸 오른쪽에 적어요.
(www.nebooks.co.kr에서 어휘 리스트를 받아 공부하세요!)

UNIT 01

현재진행형

Vocab Check! 이번 과에서 배울 단어의 뜻을 확인하고, 모르는 단어에 체크 표시하세요.

1	laugh	동 웃다	11	build	동 짓다	21	funny	형 재미있는
2	rest	동 쉬다	12	die	동 죽다	22	shine	동 빛나다
3	learn	동 배우다	13	stage	명 무대	23	together	부 함께
4	high	부 높이	14	diary	명 일기(장)	24	feed	동 먹이를 주다
5	president	명 대통령	15	use	동 사용하다	25	slowly	부 천천히
6	lie	동 눕다; 거짓말하다	16	market	명 시장	26	cucumber	명 오이
7	playground	명 놀이터	17	quietly	부 조용하게	27	spring	명 봄
8	clean	동 청소하다	18	look for	~를 찾다	28	jump	동 (제자리에서) 뛰다
9	act	동 행동하다	19	stay	동 머물다	29	lose	동 잃어버리다
10	break	동 깨다	20	bake	동 굽다	30	story	명 이야기

UNIT 01 현재진행형

I am riding my bike.
나는 자전거를 타고 있어요.

My brother is riding his bike, too.
내 남동생도 자전거를 타고 있어요.

My parents are looking at us.
나의 부모님은 우리를 보고 계세요.

A 현재진행형: ~하고 있다, ~하는 중이다

현재진행형은 'be동사 + 동사원형-ing'으로 나타내요.

I We / You / They He / She / It	**am** **are** **is**	**drinking**	water.

I **study** English every day. ⇨ I **am studying** English now.
The kids **go** to bed late at night.
⇨ The kids **are going** to bed right now.

B 동사원형-ing 만들기 참고 2권 부록

대부분의 동사	동사원형 + ing	do (하다) → do**ing** eat (먹다) → eat**ing**	play (놀다) → play**ing** buy (사다) → buy**ing**
자음 + e로 끝나는 동사	e 대신 -ing 사용	come (오다) → com**ing** write (쓰다) → writ**ing**	make (만들다) → mak**ing** dance (춤추다) → danc**ing**
-ie로 끝나는 동사	ie 대신 -ying 사용	die (죽다) → d**ying** lie (눕다, 거짓말하다) → l**ying**	
모음 1개 + 자음 1개로 끝나는 동사	끝자음 한 번 더 + -ing	sit (앉다) → sit**ting** cut (자르다) → cut**ting** swim (수영하다) → swim**ming**	run (뛰다) → run**ning**

C 현재진행형의 부정문: ~하고 있지 않다

부정문은 be동사 뒤에 not을 붙여서 'be동사 + not + 동사원형-ing'으로 나타내요.

주어	**am not** **are not[aren't]** **is not[isn't]**	**singing**	a song.

We **are staying** in a hotel now. ➾ We **are not staying** in a hotel now.

Tiffany **is listening** to music. ➾ Tiffany **isn't listening** to music.

D 현재진행형의 의문문: ~하고 있니?, ~하는 중이니?

현재진행형의 의문문은 be동사가 주어 앞으로 이동해요.

질문				대답
Am **Are** **Is**	주어	**동사원형-ing** ~?	➜	**Yes**, 주어 + **be동사**. (네, 그래요.) **No**, 주어 + **be동사** + **not**. (아니요, 그렇지 않아요.)

You **are eating** cookies.

➾ **Are** you **eating** cookies? – **Yes**, I **am**. / **No**, I'**m not**.

He **is taking** a walk.

➾ **Is** he **taking** a walk? – **Yes**, he **is**. / **No**, he **isn't**.

My Grammar Notes

1 현재진행형: be동사 + 동사원형-ing (~하는 중이다)
He runs. → He __________ __________. (현재진행형)

2 현재진행형의 부정문: be동사 + __________ + 동사원형-ing
I am reading a book. → I am __________ __________ a book. (부정문)

3 현재진행형의 의문문: be동사 + __________ + 동사원형-ing ~?
They are swimming. → __________ __________ swimming? (의문문)

Warm-Up

A 현재진행형 문장에 V 표시하세요. 현재진행형

1. He is playing basketball. V
2. I have two books.
3. The young boy is laughing.
4. Andy runs every day.
5. The polar bears are swimming.
6. Eric is learning Chinese.
7. I am looking for my bag.
8. My baby sister is sleeping.

B ( ) 안에서 알맞은 것을 고르세요. 현재진행형

1. Jack is (brush / brushing) his teeth.
2. She is (walk / walking) in the park.
3. I (study / studying) English every day.
4. The birds are (fly / flying) high in the sky.
5. The baby (smiles / smiling) a lot.
6. You are (eat / eating) too much.
7. Mike (skates / skating) every Monday.
8. The president is (make / making) a speech.

Words

laugh 웃다
polar bear 북극곰
learn 배우다
Chinese 중국어
look for ~을 찾다
brush one's teeth 양치하다
walk 걷다
park 공원
fly 날다; 날리다
high 높이
sky 하늘
smile 미소 짓다
skate 스케이트를 타다
president 대통령
make a speech 연설하다

C 부정문으로 바꿀 때 not이 들어갈 위치를 표시하세요.

현재진행형의 부정문

1. My brother is √ riding a bike.
2. I am doing my homework.
3. The children are running in the yard.
4. Jessica is cleaning her room.
5. We are singing together.
6. Tony is playing the piano.
7. She is talking on the phone.
8. Some cats are sitting on the bench.

Words

child 어린이 (복수형 **children**)
yard 마당, 뜰
clean 청소하다
together 함께
talk on the phone 전화 통화하다
bench 벤치
cry 울다
slowly 천천히
teach 가르치다
math 수학
jump (제자리에서) 뛰다

D 빈칸에 알맞은 말을 써서 의문문으로 바꾸세요.

현재진행형의 의문문

1. They are swimming. → Are they swimming ?
2. The baby is crying. → Is the baby ________ ?
3. She is going to school. → Is she ________ to school?
4. Bob is walking slowly. → ________ Bob walking slowly?
5. I am speaking fast. → Am ________ speaking fast?
6. He is teaching math. → Is ________ ________ math?
7. They are jumping high. → Are ________ ________ high?
8. We are looking for a pen. → Are we ________ for a pen?

Practice

A 다음 동사를 동사원형-ing 형태로 바꾸세요.

1. act → acting
2. cry →
3. live →
4. become →
5. begin →
6. break →
7. build →
8. say →
9. stop →
10. die →
11. sit →
12. enjoy →
13. lie →
14. cut →
15. put →
16. come →

Words

act 행동하다
live 살다
become ~이 되다
begin 시작하다
break 깨다
build 짓다
stop 멈추다
put 두다, 놓다
wait for ~를 기다리다
catch 잡다
diary 일기(장)
stage 무대
street 거리

B 주어진 동사를 이용하여 현재진행형 문장을 완성하세요.

1. Yuri is buying some fruit. (buy)
2. He ________ for Jane. (wait)
3. We ________ *Twilight*. (read)
4. Harry ________ a ball. (catch)
5. I ________ in my diary in English. (write)
6. Nicole ________ on the stage. (dance)
7. Kyle ________ down the street. (run)
8. Mom and Dad ________ breakfast. (have)

C 빈칸에 알맞은 be동사를 쓰고, 부정문으로 바꿔 쓰세요.

1. He is driving right now.
   → He isn't driving right now.
2. I ______ using the phone.
   → I ______ the phone.
3. You ______ listening to me.
   → You ______ to me.
4. It ______ snowing now.
   → It ______ now.
5. We ______ wearing jeans.
   → We ______ jeans.

Words

drive 운전하다
use 사용하다
phone 전화기
wear 입다
jeans 청바지
market 시장
grass 풀, 잔디

D 빈칸에 알맞은 be동사를 쓰고, 의문문으로 바꿔 쓰세요.

1. You are going to the market.
   → Are you going to the market?
2. Mom ______ cooking.
   → ______ cooking?
3. The boys ______ walking fast.
   → ______ walking fast?
4. They ______ lying on the grass.
   → ______ lying on the grass?
5. He ______ playing the guitar.
   → ______ playing the guitar?

E 보기에서 알맞은 말을 골라 현재진행형의 부정문을 완성하세요.

보기 play sing cook bark look ride wear

1. The boy isn't looking at you. He is looking at me.
2. We ______ quietly. We are singing loudly.
3. I ______ soup. I am cooking pasta.
4. The dog ______ at me. It is barking at you.
5. They ______ bikes. They are riding horses.
6. Kevin ______ shoes. He is wearing socks.
7. You ______ the trumpet. You are playing the flute.

Words

bark 짖다
quietly 조용하게
loudly 시끄럽게
soup 수프
pasta 파스타
ride a horse 말을 타다
socks 양말
trumpet 트럼펫
flute 플루트
stand 서다
radio 라디오

F 보기에서 알맞은 말을 골라 현재진행형의 의문문을 완성하세요.

보기 listen watch eat read use stand rain

1. Are they watching a movie? – No, they aren't.
2. ______ now? – No, it isn't.
3. ______ to the radio? – No, he isn't.
4. ______ lunch? – Yes, they are.
5. ______ under the tree? – No, she isn't.
6. ______ a comic book? – Yes, I am.
7. ______ the computer? – Yes, she is.

G 우리말과 같은 뜻이 되도록 밑줄 친 부분을 바르게 고쳐 쓰세요.

1. 우리는 아이스크림을 먹고 있다.
We eatting ice cream. → are eating

2. 그녀는 친구에게 전화를 걸고 있다.
She calls his friend. →

3. 수진이는 지하철역을 찾고 있다.
Sujin is look for a subway station. →

4. 그들은 지금 파리에 머물고 있지 않다.
They not staying in Paris now. →

5. 너 지금 숙제를 하고 있니?
Are you do your homework now? →

6. Alice가 나를 위해 빵을 굽고 있니?
Does Alice baking bread for me? →

7. Laura는 공원에서 조깅을 하고 있다.
Laura joging at the park. →

8. 그는 영화를 보고 있지 않다.
He doesn't watching a movie. →

9. Nick이 재미있는 이야기를 하고 있니?
Is Nick tells a funny story? →

10. 너는 사진을 찍고 있니?
Do you taking a picture? →

11. 그 남자들은 그 개에게 먹이를 주고 있지 않다.
The men not are feeding the dogs. →

Words

subway 지하철
station 역
stay 머물다
bake 굽다
jog 조깅하다
funny 재미있는
story 이야기
take a picture 사진을 찍다
feed 먹이를 주다

Grammar into Writing

A 우리말과 같은 뜻이 되도록 주어진 말을 이용하여 문장을 만드세요.

1. 그 소녀는 노란 장화를 신고 있다. wear yellow rain boots

→ The girl is wearing yellow rain boots.

2. 그는 신문을 읽고 있지 않다. read the newspaper

→ ______________________________

3. 그들은 영어로 이야기하고 있니? speak in English

→ ______________________________

4. Alex는 치킨 카레를 만들고 있니? make chicken curry

→ ______________________________

5. 나의 친구들이 버스를 기다리고 있다. wait for the bus

→ ______________________________

B 우리말과 같은 뜻이 되도록 주어진 말을 이용하여 문장을 완성하세요.

1. 1) 나는 영어를 배우고 있다. (learn)

→ I ___am___ ___learning___ English.

2) 내 여동생은 중국어를 배우고 있다. (Chinese)

→ My sister is learning Chinese.

2. 1) 우리는 수영장에서 수영하고 있다. (swim)

→ We __________ __________ in the pool.

2) 그들은 공원에 누워 있다. (lie, in the park)

→ ______________________________

3. 1) Susie는 음악을 듣고 있니? (listen)

→ ___________ Susie ___________ to music?

2) Chris는 컴퓨터 게임을 하고 있니? (play, a computer game)

→ ____

4. 1) David는 축구를 하고 있지 않다. (play)

→ David ___________ ___________ soccer.

2) Ted는 TV를 보고 있지 않다. (watch, TV)

→ ____

5. 1) 아이들이 치즈를 먹고 있다. (eat)

→ The kids ___________ ___________ cheese.

2) 우리는 사과 주스를 마시고 있다. (drink, apple juice)

→ ____

C 다음 글을 읽고 틀린 부분을 찾아 표시한 다음, 고쳐서 다시 써보세요.

There are some children in a park. Tom and Mina (is) playing badminton. Mike is fling a kite. Greg is rideing a bike. Jessica does going down the slide.

↓

There are some children in a park.

____

____

Words rain boots 장화 newspaper 신문 curry 카레 pool 수영장 badminton 배드민턴 kite 연 go down a slide 미끄럼틀을 타다

Wrap-Up Test

1. 동사와 동사원형-ing형이 잘못 짝지어진 것을 고르세요.

① lie – lying
② tell – telling
③ lose – losing
④ stop – stoping
⑤ cry – crying

2. 빈칸에 들어갈 수 없는 것을 고르세요.

The birds are ______________.

① fly
② flying
③ singing
④ not singing
⑤ not flying

3. 부정문으로 바꿀 때 not이 들어갈 위치를 고르세요.

John ① is ② sleeping ③ on ④ the sofa ⑤.

4. 빈칸에 알맞은 말이 바르게 짝지어진 것을 고르세요.

- I am __________ for a book.
- Lucy and I __________ going to a restaurant.

① look – am
② look – are
③ looking – am
④ looking – are
⑤ looks – are

5. 우리말을 영어로 바르게 옮긴 것을 고르세요.

너는 내 말을 듣고 있니?

① Are you listen to me?
② Are you listening to me?
③ Do you listening to me?
④ Do you listen to me?
⑤ Do you are listening to me?

Words **lose** 잃어버리다 **restaurant** 식당

정답 및 해설 p.03

6. 빈칸에 공통으로 들어갈 말을 쓰세요.

- We __________ not wearing hats.
- The students __________ reading books.

7. 밑줄 친 부분을 바르게 고친 것을 고르세요.

- Julia is <u>make</u> hamburgers.
- <u>Do</u> the children playing baseball?

① makes – Is ② makeing – Are
③ making – Are ④ makes – Are
⑤ making – Is

8. <u>틀린</u> 문장을 고르세요.

① I'm watching a quiz show.
② Is Minsu staying at home?
③ He isn't walking in the park.
④ A monkey eating bananas.
⑤ Are the boys doing their homework?

9. 올바른 문장을 고르세요.

① I cutting a cucumber.
② The frogs are jump high.
③ The girl is talks on the phone.
④ We don't running in the playground.
⑤ Is your sister cleaning the house?

10. 질문에 대한 대답으로 알맞지 <u>않은</u> 것을 고르세요.

Are you surfing the internet?

① Yes, I am.
② No, I don't.
③ No, we aren't.
④ No, I'm writing an e-mail.
⑤ Yes, I'm surfing the internet.

Words **student** 학생 **quiz show** 퀴즈쇼 **cucumber** 오이 **frog** 개구리 **playground** 놀이터 **surf the internet** 인터넷 검색을 하다

서술형

11. 빈칸에 들어갈 말이 나머지와 다른 것을 고르세요.

① Spring ________ coming slowly.

② She ________ not driving a car.

③ ________ a cat sitting on the bed?

④ ________ Andrew buying a new bag?

⑤ The stars ________ shining in the sky.

서술형

12. 질문에 대한 대답으로 알맞은 말을 빈칸에 쓰세요.

A: Are your friends writing letters?

B: No, ________ ________.

서술형

13. 우리말과 같은 뜻이 되도록 주어진 말을 바르게 배열하세요.

우리는 버스를 기다리고 있지 않다.

(not / are / a bus / we / waiting for)

→ ________________________________

____

14. 우리말과 같은 뜻이 되도록 주어진 말을 이용하여 문장을 완성하세요.

Nick은 공부하고 있지 않다. 그는 쉬는 중이다.

(study, rest)

→ Nick ________ ________

________. He ________

________.

서술형

15. 우리말과 같은 뜻이 되도록 빈칸에 알맞은 말을 쓰세요.

A: ________ Jina ________?

(지나는 수영하고 있니?)

B: No, ________ ________.

She ________ ________ a bicycle.

(아니, 그렇지 않아. 그 애는 자전거를 타고 있어.)

Words **spring** 봄 **shine** 빛나다 **letter** 편지 **rest** 쉬다 **bicycle** 자전거

UNIT 02

be동사의 과거형

Vocab Check! 이번 과에서 배울 단어의 뜻을 확인하고, 모르는 단어에 체크 표시하세요.

1	smart	형 영리한	11	mistake	명 실수	21	genius	명 천재
2	neighbor	명 이웃	12	artist	명 예술가, 화가	22	weekend	명 주말
3	excited	형 신이 난	13	hour	명 시간	23	absent	형 결석한
4	broken	형 깨진, 고장 난	14	street	명 거리	24	exciting	형 흥미진진한
5	city	명 도시	15	adult	명 성인, 어른	25	easy	형 쉬운
6	weather	명 날씨	16	polite	형 예의 바른	26	rude	형 무례한
7	sick	형 아픈	17	noisy	형 시끄러운	27	brown	형 갈색의
8	boring	형 지루한	18	choice	명 선택	28	last night	어젯밤
9	same	형 같은	19	surprised	형 놀란	29	museum	명 박물관
10	lucky	형 운이 좋은	20	lazy	형 게으른	30	heavy	형 무거운

UNIT 02 be동사의 과거형

Yesterday was moving day.
어제는 이삿날이었어요.

My family was busy. We weren't free all day.
내 가족은 바빴어요. 우리는 온종일 한가하지 않았어요.

Was I tired? – Yes, I was!
내가 피곤했느냐고요? - 네, 그랬어요!

A be동사의 현재형과 과거형

be동사의 현재형은 '~이다', '(~에) 있다'라는 뜻이고 과거형은 '~이었다', '(~에) 있었다'라는 뜻이에요.
be동사의 현재형은 am, are, is로 세 개가 있지만 과거형은 was, were 두 가지만 써요.

주어	현재		과거
I	**am**	→	was
We / You / They	**are**	→	were
He / She / It	**is**	→	was

I **am** tall now. I was short before.

It **is** warm this week. It was cold last week.

B There + be동사의 과거형: ~가 있었다

There is, There are의 과거형은 be동사를 과거형으로 바꾸어 나타내요.

There	was	+	an apple tree.	단수명사	사과 나무 한 그루가 있었어요.
			snow.	셀 수 없는 명사	눈이 있었어요.
	were		cows.	복수명사	소들이 있었어요.

There was **a large festival** last year.
(a large festival: 단수명사)

There were **many people** on the subway.
(many people: 복수명사)

C be동사 과거형의 부정문: ~이 아니었다, ~에 있지 않았다

부정의 뜻은 was, were 뒤에 not을 붙여 나타내요.

주어	was / were	not	➔	주어	wasn't / weren't

Reo was kind to me. ⇨ Reo was not[wasn't] kind to me.

They were famous singers. ⇨ They were not[weren't] famous singers.

D be동사 과거형의 의문문: ~이었니?, ~(에) 있었니?

의문문은 be동사의 과거형을 주어 앞으로 옮겨서 나타내요.

질문		➔	대답
Was / Were	주어 ~?		Yes, 주어 + was. (네, 그랬어요.) No, 주어 + wasn't. (아니요, 그렇지 않았어요.)

He was an actor. ⇨ Was he an actor?

– Yes, he was. / No, he wasn't.

You were late for school. ⇨ Were you late for school?

– Yes, we were. / No, we weren't.

Mini Grammar

과거시제에 자주 등장하는 표현

before (전에), yesterday (어제), last week (지난주), a month ago (한 달 전에), at that time (그때, 그 당시에) 등의 표현들은 과거를 나타낼 때 자주 쓰는 표현이에요. 문장에 이런 표현들이 있으면 동사는 과거형을 써야 해요.

My Grammar Notes

1 be동사의 과거형: am → ___________, are → ___________, is → ___________

2 be동사 과거형의 부정문: 주어 + was/were + not ~.
was not = wasn't / were not = ___________

3 be동사 과거형의 의문문: Was/Were + ___________ ~?
___________ he healthy? – Yes, he was. / No, he ___________.

Warm-Up

A 과거를 나타내는 문장에 V 표시하세요. be동사의 과거형

1. He was my best friend. V
2. You are very smart.
3. My aunt is a nurse.
4. I was late for school yesterday.
5. You were wonderful on the stage.
6. We were excited at the concert.
7. There was an apple on the table.
8. Tom and Jerry are my neighbors.

B ( ) 안에서 알맞은 것을 고르세요. be동사의 과거형

1. It (was / were) sunny yesterday.
2. This city (was / were) very clean.
3. They (was / were) good swimmers.
4. Jake and I (was / were) good friends.
5. My teddy bear (was / were) really cute.
6. We (was / were) very happy at that time.
7. The window (was / were) broken last week.
8. Harry and Ron (was / were) in their classroom.

Words

smart 영리한
nurse 간호사
be late for ~에 늦다
wonderful 멋진
stage 무대
excited 신이 난
concert 콘서트, 연주회
neighbor 이웃
sunny 화창한
city 도시
clean 깨끗한
swimmer 수영선수
teddy bear 곰 인형
really 정말로
broken 깨진, 고장 난
classroom 교실

C 부정문으로 바꿀 때, not이 들어갈 위치를 표시하세요.

be동사의 과거 부정문

1. The test was ✓ easy.
2. I was absent today.
3. It was cold last night.
4. Kevin was angry at me.
5. We were at the zoo yesterday.
6. There was any letter in the postbox.
7. Those shoes were my mother's.
8. The weather was good last Sunday.

Words

test 시험
easy 쉬운
absent 결석한
last night 어젯밤
angry 화가 난
zoo 동물원
postbox 우체통
weather 날씨
sick 아픈
boring 지루한
tired 피곤한
same 같은
class 반, 학급

D 빈칸에 알맞은 말을 써서 의문문으로 바꾸세요.

be동사의 과거 의문문

1. She was sick yesterday. → Was she sick yesterday?
2. I was too late. → ______ too late?
3. They were at home. → ______ at home?
4. The movie was funny. → ______ funny?
5. The books were boring. → ______ boring?
6. There were tall trees. → ______ tall trees?
7. He was tired last night. → ______ tired last night?
8. We were in the same class.
   → ______ in the same class?

Practice

A ( ) 안에서 알맞은 be동사를 고르고, 과거시제로 고쳐 쓰세요.

1. He (am / are / (is)) my teacher. → He was my teacher.
2. You (am / are / is) very lucky. → ______ very lucky.
3. They (am / are / is) dancing. → ______ dancing.
4. I (am / are / is) a student. → ______ a student.
5. We (am / are / is) hungry. → ______ hungry.
6. It (am / are / is) my mistake. → ______ my mistake.
7. She (am / are / is) an artist. → ______ an artist.

B 빈칸에 알맞은 be동사를 쓰세요.

1. Today is Monday. Yesterday was Sunday.
2. The street ______ clean now. It ______ dirty last night.
3. I ______ in my room now. I ______ in the bus an hour ago.
4. These leaves ______ red now. They ______ green before.
5. The vegetables ______ not fresh now. They ______ fresh a week ago.
6. Josh and I ______ teenagers five years ago. We ______ adults now.
7. Rob ______ 10 years old yesterday. Today, he ______ 11 years old.

Words

lucky 운이 좋은
hungry 배고픈
mistake 실수
artist 예술가, 화가
street 거리
dirty 더러운
hour 시간
leaf 잎 (복수형 **leaves**)
vegetable 채소
fresh 신선한
teenager 십 대
adult 성인, 어른

C 보기에서 알맞은 말을 골라 빈칸에 쓰세요.

보기 There is There are There was There were

1. There was a cookie on the table an hour ago.
2. ______ baseball games next week.
3. ______ roses in the garden last year.
4. ______ a good restaurant here before.
5. ______ a lot of money in my pocket now.
6. ______ many people at the party yesterday.
7. ______ many tourists at the museum last Friday.

Words

baseball game 야구 경기
rose 장미
garden 정원
restaurant 식당
pocket 주머니
tourist 관광객
museum 박물관
classmate 반 친구
library 도서관
Saturday 토요일

D 보기에서 알맞은 be동사를 골라 빈칸에 쓰세요.

보기 is are was were

1. She is very happy now.
2. I ______ tired last night.
3. Today ______ my sister's birthday.
4. They ______ at the park two hours ago.
5. Sunny and I ______ classmates this year.
6. There ______ a book under the table yesterday.
7. Yuri and Dennis ______ in the library last Saturday.

E 빈칸에 알맞은 be동사의 과거형을 쓰고, 부정문으로 고쳐 쓰세요.

1. She [was] polite. → She wasn't polite.
2. The kids [ ] noisy. → The kids ______________.
3. He [ ] a smart boy. → He ______________.
4. The men [ ] big. → The men ______________.
5. It [ ] a bad choice. → It ______________.
6. The food [ ] great. → The food ______________.
7. I [ ] surprised. → I ______________.

Words

polite 예의 바른
noisy 시끄러운
choice 선택
surprised 놀란
lazy 게으른
kind 친절한
everyone 모든 사람
snack 간식
tasty 맛있는

F 의문문으로 바꾸고, 대답을 완성하세요.

1. The room was clean.
   → [Was the room] clean? – No, [it wasn't].
2. They were good singers.
   → [ ] good singers? – Yes, [ ].
3. The dress was really nice.
   → [ ] really nice? – Yes, [ ].
4. He was lazy before.
   → [ ] lazy before? – No, [ ].
5. She was kind to everyone.
   → [ ] kind to everyone? – Yes, [ ].
6. The snacks were tasty.
   → [ ] tasty? – No, [ ].

G 우리말과 같은 뜻이 되도록 문장을 완성하세요.

1. 너는 그때 7살이었어.
   → You ___were___ 7 years old at that time.
2. 아인슈타인은 천재였다.
   → Einstein ______ a genius.
3. Cindy는 지난 주말에 집에 있었니?
   → ______ Cindy at home last weekend?
4. 우리 부모님은 한국에서 태어나시지 않았다.
   → My parents ______ born in Korea.
5. 그 스테이크는 맛있었니?
   → ______ the steak delicious?
6. 그는 몇 년 전에는 유명하지 않았다.
   → He ______ famous a few years ago.
7. 우리는 Lee 선생님의 학생들이었다.
   → We ______ Mr. Lee's students.
8. 교실은 아주 조용했다.
   → The classroom ______ very quiet.
9. 그 게임은 정말로 흥미진진했다.
   → The game ______ really exciting.
10. 냉장고에 우유가 조금도 없었다.
    → There ______ any milk in the refrigerator.
11. 놀이공원에 사람들이 많이 있었니?
    → ______ there many people at the amusement park?

Words

genius 천재
weekend 주말
parents 부모님
be born 태어나다
delicious 맛있는
famous 유명한
quiet 조용한
exciting 흥미진진한
refrigerator 냉장고
amusement park 놀이공원

Grammar into Writing

A **우리말과 같은 뜻이 되도록 주어진 말을 이용하여 문장을 만드세요.**

1. 바람이 아주 차가웠다. the wind / very cold
→ The wind was very cold.

2. 그의 손은 따뜻했다. hands / warm
→ ____________________

3. 열쇠는 테이블 아래에 없었다. the key / under the table
→ ____________________

4. 너는 도서관에 있었니? you / at the library
→ ____________________

5. 날씨가 좋았니? the weather / good
→ ____________________

B **우리말과 같은 뜻이 되도록 주어진 말을 이용하여 문장을 완성하세요.**

1. 1) John은 어제 아팠다.
→ John __was__ sick yesterday.
2) 우리는 어제 슬펐다. (sad)
→ We were sad yesterday.

2. 1) 수업은 지루하지 않았다.
→ The class ________ boring.
2) 그 사람들은 졸리지 않았다. (the people, sleepy)
→ ____________________

3. 1) 교실에 30명의 학생이 있었다.

→ There __________ thirty students in the classroom.

2) 교실에 시계가 하나 있었다. (a clock)

→ ______________________________________

4. 1) 나는 지난주에 부산에 있었다.

→ I __________ in Busan last week.

2) 부모님은 지난주에 서울에 계셨다. (my parents, Seoul)

→ ______________________________________

5. 1) 넌 그날 화가 났었니?

→ __________ you angry that day?

2) 너의 컴퓨터는 그날 고장 났었니? (your computer, broken)

→ ______________________________________

C 다음 글을 읽고 빈칸에 알맞은 be동사를 넣은 후, 우리말로 해석하세요.

Jina and I are good friends, but we are very different. Jina ___is___ short, but I _________ tall. Jina is good at math, but I'm not. There _________ a math test in school yesterday. It was very easy for Jina. _________ it easy for me? No, it _________!

↓

지나와 나는 ______________________________________

____

____

Words wind 바람 hand 손 warm 따뜻한 key 열쇠 sleepy 졸린 clock 시계 different 다른 be good at ~를 잘하다 math test 수학 시험

Wrap-Up Test

1. 대명사 주어와 be동사의 과거형이 바르게 연결되지 않은 것을 고르세요.

① I – was ② you – was

③ he – was ④ they – were

⑤ it – was

2. 부정문으로 바꿀 때 not이 들어갈 위치를 고르세요.

Neil ① was ② a ③ rude ④ student ⑤.

[3-4] 빈칸에 들어갈 수 없는 것을 고르세요.

3.

This cake __________ sweet.

① was ② isn't

③ are ④ wasn't

⑤ is

4.

We were in Seoul ______________.

① before ② now

③ yesterday ④ last week

⑤ six hours ago

5. 빈칸에 알맞은 말을 고르세요.

I __________ late for school yesterday.

① am ② were

③ wasn't ④ weren't

⑤ is

6. 질문에 대한 대답으로 빈칸에 알맞은 말을 쓰세요.

A: Was the test difficult yesterday? B: No, __________ __________.

Words **rude** 무례한 **sweet** 달콤한 **difficult** 어려운

7. 빈칸에 알맞은 말이 바르게 짝지어진 것을 고르세요.

- Billy _________ in my class last year.
- We _________ good friends now.

① is – are ② is – were
③ was – are ④ was – were
⑤ were – are

8. 질문에 대한 대답으로 알맞지 <u>않은</u> 것을 고르세요.

Was he your English teacher last year?

① Yes, he was.
② Yes, he wasn't.
③ No, he wasn't.
④ No, he was my math teacher.
⑤ Yes, he was my English teacher.

9. 우리말을 영어로 바르게 옮긴 것을 고르세요.

Andrew는 예전에 키가 크지 않았다.

① Andrew isn't tall before.
② Andrew wasn't tall before.
③ Andrew were not tall before.
④ Andrew does not tall before.
⑤ Andrew are not tall before.

10. 빈칸에 들어갈 말이 나머지와 <u>다른</u> 것을 고르세요.

① I _______ not busy last Friday.
② _______ it windy two hours ago?
③ _______ your uncle a scientist before?
④ The movie last weekend _______ interesting.
⑤ Alex and I _______ at the museum yesterday.

Words **busy** 바쁜 **windy** 바람이 부는 **scientist** 과학자 **interesting** 흥미로운

11. 틀린 문장을 고르세요.

① Her hair was brown.

② The boys were short and big.

③ The book were not popular.

④ Kelly was in Paris last month.

⑤ There were many trees in the garden.

12. 대화가 어색한 것을 고르세요.

① A: Was it cold last month?
B: Yes, it was.

② A: Was he born in Korea?
B: No, he wasn't.

③ A: Were you at the theater that day?
B: Yes, I was.

④ A: Were they at the playground?
B: No, they was not.

⑤ A: Were your parents tired last night?
B: Yes, they were.

서술형

13. 틀린 부분을 찾아 바르게 고쳐 쓰세요.

My pets are sick a week ago.

__________ → __________

서술형

14. 우리말과 같은 뜻이 되도록 주어진 말을 바르게 배열하세요.

몇 년 전에는 공원에 연못이 없었다.
(a pond / there / not / was)

→ ______________________________
in the park a few years ago.

서술형

15. 우리말과 같은 뜻이 되도록 대화를 완성하세요. (빈칸에 한 단어씩 쓸 것)

A: __________ the boxes heavy?
(그 상자들은 무거웠니?)
B: Yes. They __________ light.
(응. 그것들은 가볍지 않았어.)

Words brown 갈색의 popular 인기 있는 Paris (프랑스) 파리 theater 극장 playground 놀이터 pond 연못 heavy 무거운 light 가벼운

UNIT 03

일반동사의 과거형

Vocab Check! 이번 과에서 배울 단어의 뜻을 확인하고, 모르는 단어에 체크 표시하세요.

1	handsome	형 잘생긴	11	travel	동 여행하다	21	ride	동 타다
2	send	동 보내다	12	plant	동 심다	22	puzzle	명 퍼즐
3	job	명 일, 직업	13	foreigner	명 외국인	23	win	동 이기다
4	wallet	명 지갑	14	usually	부 보통, 대개	24	present	명 선물
5	pass	동 통과하다	15	rice	명 쌀; 밥	25	begin	동 시작하다
6	minute	명 (시간) 분	16	hurt	동 다치게 하다	26	drop	동 떨어뜨리다
7	password	명 비밀번호	17	gym	명 체육관	27	store	명 가게
8	dish	명 접시	18	fail	동 실패하다	28	weekday	명 평일
9	address	명 주소	19	magazine	명 잡지	29	healthy	형 건강한
10	plan	동 계획하다	20	fight	동 싸우다	30	spaghetti	명 스파게티

UNIT 03 일반동사의 과거형

World War II began **in 1939.**
1939년에 제2차 세계 대전이 시작됐어요.

Many people died **in the war.**
많은 사람이 그 전쟁에서 죽었어요.

Now, we want peace in the world.
이제, 우리는 세계에 평화를 원해요.

A 현재형 (~하다) *vs.* 과거형 (~했다)

일반동사의 현재형은 주어에 따라 형태가 바뀌지만, 과거형은 주어와 상관없이 형태가 같아요.

주어	일반동사(현재)	일반동사(과거)
I	**smile.**	
He / She / It	**smiles.**	→ smiled. (미소 지었다)
We / You / They	**smile.** (미소 짓다)	

I often **play** soccer. I played soccer yesterday.
(나는 종종 축구를 해요. 나는 어제 축구를 했어요.)

She **exercises** every day. She exercised last night.
(그녀는 매일 운동해요. 그녀는 어젯밤에 운동했어요.)

We sometimes **fight**. We fought two hours ago.
(우리는 가끔 싸워요. 우리는 두 시간 전에 싸웠어요.)

Mini Grammar 참고 UNIT 02

항상 과거시제를 사용하는 경우

1. 과거를 나타내는 시간의 부사구가 쓰인 경우

I cleaned my room yesterday. (나는 어제 내 방을 청소했어요.)

2. 역사적 사건을 말할 경우

Mozart was born in 1756. (모차르트는 1756년에 태어났어요.)

B 일반동사의 과거형 만들기

1. 규칙적인 과거형 참고 2권 부록

대부분의 동사	동사원형 + ed	help (돕다) → help**ed** want (원하다) → want**ed** talk (말하다) → talk**ed**
자음 + e로 끝나는 동사	동사원형 + d	like (좋아하다) → like**d** move (옮기다) → move**d** hope (바라다) → hope**d** believe (믿다) → believe**d**
자음 + y로 끝나는 동사	y 대신 -ied 사용	cry (울다) → cr**ied** study (공부하다) → stud**ied**
모음 1개 + 자음 1개로 끝나는 동사	끝자음 한 번 더 + ed	stop (멈추다) → stop**ped** drop (떨어뜨리다) → drop**ped**

'모음+y'로 끝나는 동사는 끝에 -ed를 붙여요.
play (놀다) → played

2. 불규칙한 과거형 참고 2권 부록

1) 현재형과 과거형의 형태가 다른 동사

do (하다) → **did**
see (보다) → **saw**
come (오다) → **came**
know (알다) → **knew**
tell (말하다) → **told**

go (가다) → **went**
have (가지다) → **had**
make (만들다) → **made**
meet (만나다) → **met**
sit (앉다) → **sat**

run (뛰다) → **ran**
eat (먹다) → **ate**
give (주다) → **gave**
buy (사다) → **bought**
get (받다, 얻다) → **got**

2) 현재형과 과거형의 형태가 같은 동사

cut (자르다) → **cut**
hurt (다치게 하다) → **hurt**

put (놓다, 두다) → **put**
read (읽다) → **read**

read는 현재형과 과거형의 발음이 달라요.
현재형: [ri:d] 과거형: [réd]

My Grammar Notes

1 과거에 일어난 일을 나타낼 때는 동사의 ____________을 쓴다.

2 과거형의 규칙 변화: want → ____________ live → ____________
cry → ____________ stop → ____________

3 과거형의 불규칙 변화: do → ____________ come → ____________
read → ____________ give → ____________

Warm-Up

A 과거를 나타내는 문장에 V 표시하세요. 현재형 / 과거형

1.	I met my friend yesterday.	V
2.	He goes swimming every Monday.	
3.	Mary bought a hat last Thursday.	
4.	It is raining now.	
5.	Daniel is handsome and kind.	
6.	The woman was a fashion model.	
7.	I got up early this morning.	
8.	He always fights with his sister.	
9.	My uncle lives in New York.	
10.	My brother is surfing the internet.	
11.	He sent five e-mails this afternoon.	
12.	We were 10 years old in 2005.	
13.	The man is watching TV.	
14.	I saw a movie last night.	
15.	Harry started the job two years ago.	
16.	Now I read a lot of books.	
17.	Michelle lost her wallet last week.	
18.	He is writing a letter to Mike.	

Words

handsome 잘생긴
model 모델
fight 싸우다
surf the internet 인터넷 검색을 하다
send 보내다 (과거형 **sent**)
job 일, 직업
lose 잃어버리다 (과거형 **lost**)
wallet 지갑
letter 편지

B 동사의 과거형을 골라 O 표시하세요. 과거형 만들기

looked	sat	live	told
bring	likes	studying	drop
cried	need	wanted	running
made	visit	watches	open
meet	get	came	did

Words

bring 가져오다
visit 방문하다
open 열다
plan 계획하다
hear 듣다

C 알맞은 과거형을 고르세요. 과거형 만들기

1. go (goed / went)
2. play (plaied / played)
3. take (taked / took)
4. buy (bought / buied)
5. hope (hoped / hopped)
6. fight (fighted / fought)
7. give (gived / gave)
8. hurt (hurt / hurted)
9. stop (stoped / stopped)
10. smile (smileed / smiled)
11. say (sayed / said)
12. read (red / read)
13. have (had / haved)
14. know (knowed / knew)
15. dance (danced / danceed)
16. talk (talked / talkd)
17. eat (eated / ate)
18. plan (planed / planned)
19. cut (cutted / cut)
20. hear (heared / heard)

Practice

A 규칙 변화를 하는 동사입니다. 과거형으로 바꿔 쓰세요.

1. watch	→	watched	2. enjoy	→	
3. love	→		4. visit	→	
5. stop	→		6. help	→	
7. fail	→		8. try	→	
9. work	→		10. hate	→	
11. pass	→		12. talk	→	
13. wash	→		14. jump	→	

B 불규칙 변화를 하는 동사입니다. 과거형으로 바꿔 쓰세요.

1. meet	→	met	2. give	→	
3. sing	→		4. run	→	
5. drive	→		6. sit	→	
7. come	→		8. drink	→	
9. sleep	→		10. have	→	
11. swim	→		12. write	→	
13. find	→		14. make	→	
15. lose	→		16. teach	→	
17. get	→		18. put	→	

Words

fail 실패하다
try 시도하다
work 일하다
hate 싫어하다
pass 통과하다
wash 씻다
drive 운전하다
drink 마시다
find 찾다
teach 가르치다

C ( ) 안에서 알맞은 것을 고르세요.

1. I (listen / listened) to music at night these days.
   I (listen / listened) to jazz last night.

2. I (eat / ate) spaghetti at a restaurant last Sunday.
   I (eat / ate) spaghetti on Sundays.

3. I (go / went) shopping once a week.
   I (go / went) shopping with my mom yesterday.

4. Greg's room is clean. He (cleans / cleaned) it every day.
   He (cleans / cleaned) his room two hours ago.

5. Anna likes movies. She (sees / saw) a movie every Friday.
   Anna and I (see / saw) the movie *Avengers* last Friday.

6. He (exercises / exercised) every day, so he is healthy.
   He (exercises / exercised) with his brother yesterday.

7. He gets up early because his class (begins / began) at 8.
   The class (begins / began) 10 minutes late this morning.

8. Amy is my best friend. I (know / knew) her well.
   I (know / knew) her password, but now I forgot it.

9. I (play / played) the piano with my brother last week.
   I usually (play / played) the piano with my sister.

10. My mom (buys / bought) a present for me every year.
    She (buy / bought) me a new smartphone last year.

Words

jazz (음악) 재즈
spaghetti 스파게티
go shopping 쇼핑하러 가다
once a week 일주일에 한 번
clean 깨끗한; 청소하다
exercise 운동하다
healthy 건강한
because ~ 때문에
begin 시작하다 (과거형 **began**)
minute (시간) 분
password 비밀번호
forget 잊어버리다 (과거형 **forgot**)
usually 보통, 대개
present 선물
smartphone 스마트폰

D 주어진 단어를 과거형으로 바꾸어 문장을 완성하세요.

1. call — Emily **called** me last night.
2. drop — Paul ______ the dish.
3. dance — We ______ at the party.
4. cry — The baby ______ all night.
5. wait — I ______ for Henry for an hour.
6. have — Amy ______ lunch with her friend.
7. play — We ______ basketball after school.
8. come — He ______ back to Korea a few days ago.

Words

dish 접시
wait for ~를 기다리다
basketball 농구
come back to ~로 돌아오다
plant 심다
travel 여행하다
address 주소
soda 탄산음료
all over the world 전 세계 곳곳에
foreigner 외국인
Arbor Day 식목일
yard 마당

E 보기에서 알맞은 단어를 골라 과거형으로 바꾸어 문장을 완성하세요.

보기 drink plant speak meet travel know eat

1. They **met** at the park.
2. My uncle ______ my address.
3. He ______ too much soda last night.
4. The woman ______ all over the world.
5. A foreigner ______ to me on the street.
6. My brother ______ five pieces of pizza.
7. On Arbor Day, we ______ some trees in the yard.

F 주어진 단어를 이용하여 문장을 완성하세요. 필요하면 형태를 바꾸세요.

1. be — I was born 13 years ago. / I am 13 years old now.

2. go — Julia usually ______ to bed at 10. / She ______ to bed at 12 last night.

3. teach — My mom ______ music three years ago. / Now she ______ piano.

4. have — She usually ______ rice for breakfast. / She ______ bread yesterday morning.

5. live — My family ______ in Seoul last year. / We ______ in Tokyo now.

6. wake — My father usually ______ up at 6 a.m. / He ______ up at 8 a.m. yesterday.

7. want — Jack ______ to be an actor last year. / Now he ______ to be a singer.

8. read — He ______ *Alice in Wonderland* last week. / Now he is ______ *The Little Prince*.

9. open — The store usually ______ at 10 on weekdays. / But the store ______ at 11 last Monday.

10. play — Joel often ______ tennis in the morning. / Joel is ______ tennis with me right now.

Words

rice 쌀; 밥
wake up 일어나다
actor (남자) 배우
Alice in Wonderland 「이상한 나라의 앨리스」
The Little Prince 「어린왕자」
store 가게
weekday 평일

Grammar into Writing

A 소희가 지난 일주일 동안 한 일을 나타낸 메모를 보고, 빈칸에 알맞은 말을 쓰세요.

Monday: watch TV
Tuesday: meet Jessica
Wednesday: make cookies
Thursday: study English
Friday: see a movie
Saturday: write e-mails
Sunday: go shopping

1. She ___watched TV___ on Monday.
2. She ______________ on Tuesday.
3. She ______________ on Wednesday.
4. She ______________ on Thursday.
5. She ______________ on Friday.
6. She ______________ on Saturday.
7. She ______________ on Sunday.

B 우리말과 같은 뜻이 되도록 주어진 말을 이용하여 문장을 완성하세요.

1. 1) 1월에는 눈이 많이 온다. (snow)

→ It ___snows___ a lot in January.

2) 지난달에는 눈이 많이 왔다. (last month)

→ ___It snowed a lot last month.___

2. 1) 그녀는 종종 나를 집까지 차로 데려다준다. (drive)

→ She often __________ me home.

2) 그는 어젯밤에 우리를 집까지 차로 데려다주었다. (last night)

→ ______________________________

3. 1) Alex는 항상 나를 도와준다. (help)

→ Alex always __________ me.

2) 우리는 지난주에 그를 도와주었다. (last week)

→ ______________________________

4. 1) 나는 매일 책을 읽는다. (read)

→ I __________ a book every day.

2) Jack은 어제 책을 읽었다. (yesterday)

→ ______________________________

5. 1) 내 동생은 매주 피아노 강습을 받는다. (take)

→ My sister __________ piano lessons every week.

2) 나는 2년 전에 피아노 강습을 받았다. (two years ago)

→ ______________________________

C 다음 글을 읽고 틀린 부분을 찾아 표시한 다음, 고쳐서 다시 써보세요.

I went to an amusement park with my little brother yesterday. We ride the roller coaster and the merry-go-round. We eat pizza and drink Coke. We have a great time!

↓

I went to ______________________________

____

____

Words **drive** (차로) 데려다주다 **lesson** 수업, 교습 **amusement park** 놀이공원 **ride** 타다 **roller coaster** 롤러코스터 **merry-go-round** 회전목마

Wrap-Up Test

1. 동사의 현재형과 과거형이 잘못 짝지어진 것을 고르세요.

① cry – cried ② drop – droped
③ have – had ④ make – made
⑤ leave – left

2. 동사의 현재형과 과거형의 형태가 다른 것을 고르세요.

① put ② cut ③ read
④ sit ⑤ hurt

3. 빈칸에 알맞은 것을 고르세요.

We ______________ China in 2015.

① visit ② visits
③ is visiting ④ are visiting
⑤ visited

[4-5] 빈칸에 알맞은 말이 바르게 짝지어진 것을 고르세요.

4.

Brian usually __________ a bus to school, but he __________ a taxi yesterday.

① take – took ② takes – takes
③ takes – took ④ took – takes
⑤ took – take

5.

- I __________ him at the gym before.
- She __________ to bed at 11 p.m. last night.

① see – go ② saw – went
③ see – went ④ saw – goes
⑤ see – goes

Words **take a bus** 버스를 타다 **gym** 체육관

6. 밑줄 친 부분을 바르게 고친 것을 고르세요.

- I starts the job in 2012.
- Jeff give me a ring a month ago.

① started – gives ② start – gived
③ started – gived ④ started – gave
⑤ start – gave

[7-8] 빈칸에 들어갈 수 없는 것을 고르세요.

7.

Andy painted the door ______________.

① now ② this afternoon
③ at 11 ④ an hour ago
⑤ at that time

8.

She ____________________ last week.

① had ice cream
② read a magazine
③ drove the car fast
④ fights with her sister
⑤ heard the news

9. 우리말을 영어로 바르게 옮긴 것을 고르세요.

나는 어제 Joe를 위한 선물을 샀다.

① I buy a present for Joe yesterday.
② I buys a present for Joe yesterday.
③ I buyed a present for Joe yesterday.
④ I bought a present for Joe yesterday.
⑤ I am buying a present for Joe yesterday.

10. 밑줄 친 부분이 어색한 것을 고르세요.

① I lost my dog at the zoo.
② Brian got up late this morning.
③ She finished the puzzle last night.
④ World War II ended in 1945.
⑤ They win the basketball game yesterday.

Words
ring 반지 **paint** 페인트 칠하다 **magazine** 잡지 **finish** 끝내다, 완성하다
puzzle 퍼즐 **World War II** 제2차 세계 대전 **end** 끝나다 **win** 이기다

11. 올바른 문장을 고르세요.

① It rain a lot two hours ago.

② She meeted her uncle last week.

③ Anna lives in Hong Kong before.

④ He found my bag on the bench yesterday.

⑤ The lesson begined at 7 p.m. last Thursday.

[12-13] 틀린 부분을 찾아 바르게 고쳐 쓰세요.

서술형

12.

She swimed in the sea last summer vacation.

________ → ________

서술형

13.

Kevin does his homework well last night.

________ → ________

서술형

14. 우리말과 같은 뜻이 되도록 주어진 말을 이용하여 문장을 완성하세요.

그는 지난 주말에 부모님을 도와드렸다.
(help his parents)

→ ________________ last weekend.

서술형

15. 일반동사의 과거형을 찾아 차례대로 빈칸에 쓰고, 각각의 동사원형을 쓰세요.

It was Laura's birthday a few days ago. Her friends came to the party and sang "Happy Birthday" to her. She got many presents.

〈과거형〉 〈동사원형〉

(1) ________ – ________

(2) ________ – ________

(3) ________ – ________

Words summer vacation 여름방학 weekend 주말 a few days 며칠

UNIT 04

일반동사 과거형의 부정문과 의문문

Vocab Check! 이번 과에서 배울 단어의 뜻을 확인하고, 모르는 단어에 체크 표시하세요.

1	beach	명 해변	11	flight	명 비행, 항공편	21	borrow	동 빌리다
2	invite	동 초대하다	12	miss	동 놓치다	22	library	명 도서관
3	secret	명 비밀	13	turn on	~을 켜다	23	make fun of	~을 놀리다
4	Beijing	명 (중국) 베이징	14	light	명 전등	24	football	명 미식축구
5	airport	명 공항	15	dinner	명 저녁 식사	25	interesting	형 흥미로운
6	lock	동 잠그다	16	on time	제때, 제시간에	26	go out	외출하다
7	face	명 얼굴	17	pool	명 수영장	27	eat out	외식하다
8	fix	동 고치다, 수리하다	18	gift	명 선물	28	festival	명 축제
9	answer	명 정답	19	mall	명 쇼핑몰	29	snowman	명 눈사람
10	schoolbag	명 책가방	20	scary	형 무서운	30	river	명 강

UNIT 04 일반동사 과거형의 부정문과 의문문

My friends and I did homework together.
내 친구들과 나는 함께 숙제를 했어요.

My friends didn't finish theirs.
내 친구들은 그들의 것을 끝내지 않았어요.

Did I finish mine? – Yes, I did!
제 것을 끝냈느냐고요? – 네, 그랬어요!

A 일반동사 과거형의 부정문: ~하지 않았다

일반동사 과거형의 부정문은 동사원형 앞에 did not을 사용해서 나타내요.

주어	did not[didn't] (~하지 않았다)	동사원형 ~.

did는 주어에 따라 형태가 변하지 않아요.

I **watched** TV late at night. → I did not watch TV late at night.
= I didn't watch TV late at night.
(나는 밤늦게 TV를 보지 않았어요.)

He **did** his laundry. → He did not do his laundry.
= He didn't do his laundry.
(그는 빨래를 하지 않았어요.)

We **went** to school yesterday. → We did not go to school yesterday.
= We didn't go to school yesterday.
(우리는 어제 학교에 가지 않았어요.)

Mini Grammar 참고 1권 Unit 10

일반동사 현재형의 부정문: 주어+don't[doesn't]+동사원형
I **don't** drink coffee. (나는 커피를 마시지 않아요.)
She **doesn't** drink coffee. (그녀는 커피를 마시지 않아요.)

B 일반동사 과거형의 의문문: ~했니?

일반동사 과거형의 의문문은 did를 문장 맨 앞에 써서 나타내요.

질문				대답
Did	주어	동사원형?	→	Yes, 주어 + did. (네, 그랬어요.) No, 주어 + didn't. (아니요, 그렇지 않았어요.)

You **enjoyed** the movie. ⇨ Did you enjoy the movie?
(당신은 그 영화를 즐겼나요?)
– Yes, I did. / No, I didn't.

He **slept** on the sofa. ⇨ Did he sleep on the sofa?
(그는 소파에서 잤나요?)
– Yes, he did. / No, he didn't.

Tom and Jane **got** married last year.
⇨ Did Tom and Jane get married last year?
(Tom과 Jane은 작년에 결혼했나요?)
– Yes, they did. / No, they didn't.

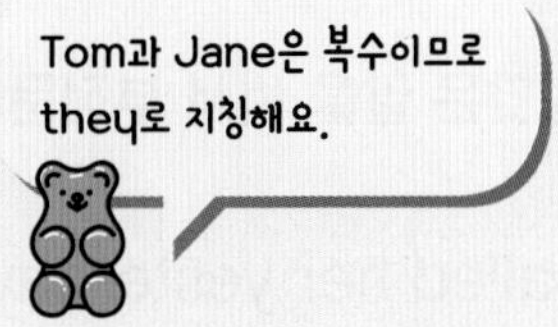

Mini Grammar 참고 1권 Unit 10

일반동사 현재형의 의문문: Do[Does] + 주어 + 동사원형 ~?
Do you know the answer? (당신은 정답을 아나요?)
Does he know the answer? (그는 정답을 아나요?)

My Grammar Notes

1 일반동사 과거형의 부정문: 주어 + ____________ + ____________ + 동사원형 ~.
그녀는 그 치마를 사지 않았다. → She ____________ buy the skirt.

2 일반동사 과거형의 의문문: ____________ + 주어 + 동사원형 ~?
너는 손을 씻었니? → ____________ you wash your hands?

3 일반동사 과거형의 부정문과 의문문은 주어에 상관없이 do[does]의 과거형인 ____________를 이용하여 나타낸다.

Warm-Up

A 빈칸에 알맞은 말을 보기에서 골라 쓰세요. 일반동사의 부정문

보기	don't	doesn't	didn't

1. She didn't go to the beach last Sunday.
2. We ______ have any money now.
3. I ______ meet my friend yesterday.
4. My brother ______ live in Korea now.
5. Sam ______ play computer games last week.

Words

beach 해변
call 전화하다
do one's laundry 빨래하다
secret 비밀
keep a diary 일기를 쓰다

B 빈칸에 알맞은 말을 써서 부정문을 완성하세요. 일반동사의 과거 부정문

1. Noah called her yesterday.
→ Noah didn't call her yesterday.
2. She did her laundry.
→ She ______ ______ her laundry.
3. I told her the secret.
→ I ______ ______ her the secret.
4. It rained yesterday.
→ It ______ ______ yesterday.
5. Nicky kept a diary last year.
→ Nicky ______ ______ a diary last year.
6. My father watched the news at that time.
→ My father ______ ______ the news at that time.

C 빈칸에 알맞은 말을 써서 의문문을 완성하세요. 일반동사의 의문문

1. She went to Beijing last summer.
   → Did she go to Beijing last summer?
2. He drank some milk this morning.
   → ______ he ______ some milk this morning?
3. He bought the book yesterday.
   → ______ he ______ the book yesterday?
4. They take an exam once a month.
   → ______ they ______ an exam once a month?
5. Mia does her homework after dinner.
   → ______ Mia ______ her homework after dinner?
6. My aunt arrived at the airport an hour ago.
   → ______ my aunt ______ at the airport an hour ago?

Words

Beijing (중국) 베이징
take an exam 시험을 보다
arrive at ~에 도착하다
airport 공항
bark 짖다
present 선물
text message 문자 메시지
go camping 캠핑 가다

D 의문문에 대한 대답을 완성하세요. 일반동사의 과거 의문문

1. Did you sleep well last night? – Yes, I did.
2. Did the dog bark at him? – Yes, ______.
3. Did your friends call you? – No, ______.
4. Did Alice like the present? – Yes, ______.
5. Did you get my text message? – No, ______.
6. Did he go camping last weekend? – No, ______.

Practice

A 보기의 단어를 이용하여 과거시제의 의문문을 완성하세요.

보기 take wash sing drink read

1. Did she take a shower?
2. ______ Brian ______ his hands?
3. ______ he ______ the book?
4. ______ you ______ the tea?
5. ______ they ______ a birthday song?

B 주어진 단어를 이용하여 문장을 완성하세요. 필요하면 형태를 바꾸세요.

1. meet
   I met Mike yesterday.
   I didn't meet Anna.
2. play
   Tony ______ baseball last Sunday.
   He didn't ______ football.
3. have
   He ______ pizza for lunch an hour ago.
   He didn't ______ pickles.
4. fix
   My father ______ the computer yesterday.
   He didn't ______ the clock.
5. teach
   Lisa ______ math at school last year.
   She didn't ______ English.

Words

wash 씻다
take a shower 샤워하다
football 미식축구
pickle 피클
fix 고치다, 수리하다
clock 시계

C 빈칸에 알맞은 말을 써서 부정문과 의문문을 각각 완성하세요.

1. Sara went to the zoo yesterday.
   → Sara didn't go the zoo yesterday.
   → Did Sara go to the zoo yesterday?
2. He wanted a new schoolbag.
   → ______ a new schoolbag.
   → ______ a new schoolbag?
3. They brought sandwiches for lunch.
   → ______ sandwiches for lunch.
   → ______ sandwiches for lunch?
4. We invited you to dinner.
   → ______ you to dinner.
   → ______ you to dinner?
5. He missed the first bus.
   → ______ the first bus.
   → ______ the first bus?
6. The train left on time.
   → ______ on time.
   → ______ on time?
7. The children broke the window.
   → ______ the window.
   → ______ the window?
8. You wore a red dress at the party.
   → ______ a red dress at the party.
   → ______ a red dress at the party?

Words

schoolbag 책가방
bring 가져오다 (과거형 **brought**)
invite 초대하다
miss 놓치다
leave 떠나다 (과거형 **left**)
on time 제때, 제시간에
wear 입다 (과거형 **wore**)

D 다음은 Jack이 지난 일요일에 한 일입니다. 표의 내용에 맞게 대화를 완성하세요.

10 a.m.	get up	6 p.m.	have dinner
12 p.m.	play soccer with his friend Peter	8 p.m.	read a book
2 p.m.	go to a fast-food restaurant	9 p.m.	take a bath with his dad
4 p.m.	do homework	10 p.m.	go to bed

1. Did you get up early last Sunday, Jack?
   – No, I didn't. I got up at 10 a.m.
2. Did you take a shower in the morning?
   – No, but I ______ a bath at night.
3. Did you meet your friend that day?
   – Yes, I did. I met Peter, and we ______ soccer.
4. Did you have lunch at home?
   – No, I ______. I ______ to a fast-food restaurant.
5. Did you ______ your homework?
   – Yes, ______ ______ it at 4 p.m.
6. Did you study English?
   – No, but I ______ a book.
7. Did you take a bath last night?
   – ______, I ______. I did it with my dad.
8. Did you go to bed at 11 p.m.?
   – ______, I ______ to bed at 10 p.m.

Words

fast-food restaurant 패스트푸드점
dinner 저녁 식사
take a bath 목욕하다
go to bed 잠자리에 들다

E 주어진 단어를 이용하여 과거시제 문장을 완성하세요.

1. She didn't read his letter. (not, read)
2. The concert ______ last week. (start)
   And it ______ today. (not, end)
3. They ______ in the river yesterday. (not, swim)
   They ______ in the pool. (swim)
4. A: ______ Tommy ______ the candy? (eat)
   B: No, he didn't. His brother ______ it. (eat)
5. A: ______ Jina ______ to the baseball game? (go)
   B: Yes, she did. She ______ the game. (enjoy)

Words

letter 편지
concert 콘서트, 음악회
end 끝나다
river 강
pool 수영장
enjoy 즐기다
go fishing 낚시하러 가다
pass 통과하다
gift 선물
alone 혼자서
mall 쇼핑몰

F 밑줄 친 부분을 바르게 고쳐 쓰세요.

1. Do you go fishing yesterday? → Did you go
2. Did she passed the test? → ______
3. Did your mom likes your gift? → ______
4. I don't have pasta last Monday. → ______
5. She didn't rode a bike this morning. → ______
6. Did you make the chocolate alone?
   – No, you didn't. → ______
7. Did he buy his shoes at the mall?
   – No, he doesn't. → ______

Grammar into Writing

A 우리말과 같은 뜻이 되도록 보기에서 알맞은 말을 골라 문장을 만드세요.

보기			
	take a bus	fight with his friend	make a snowman
	walk my dog	go to the museum	run down the street

1. 그녀는 버스를 타지 않았다. → She didn't take a bus.
2. 그는 어제 박물관에 가지 않았다. → ______________________
3. Daniel이 친구랑 싸웠니? → ______________________
4. 너희들은 눈사람을 만들었니? → ______________________

B 우리말과 같은 뜻이 되도록 주어진 말을 이용하여 문장을 완성하세요.

1. 1) 그는 어제 일하러 가지 않았다. (go)
   → He didn't go to work yesterday.
   2) 나는 어제 학교에 가지 않았다. (school)
   → I didn't go to school yesterday.
2. 1) 너는 그 편지를 읽었니? (read)
   → ________ you ________ the letter?
   2) 그는 오늘자 신문을 읽었니? (today's newspaper)
   → ______________________
3. 1) Billy는 세수를 하지 않았다. (wash)
   → Billy ________ ________ his face.
   2) 우리 아빠는 세차를 하지 않았다. (his car)
   → ______________________

4. 1) 그는 나의 이름을 잊어버렸니? (forget)

→ __________ he __________ my name?

2) 그녀는 너의 생일을 잊어버렸니? (your birthday)

→ ______________________________

5. 1) 우리는 창문을 잠그지 않았다. (lock)

→ We __________ __________ the window.

2) 그들은 문을 잠그지 않았다. (the door)

→ ______________________________

C 다음 대화를 읽고 틀린 부분을 찾아 표시한 다음, 고쳐서 다시 써보세요.

A: I'm so tired. I don't sleep last night.
B: Did you played games all night?
A: No, I did. I don't play games now.
B: What did you do yesterday?
A: I see a horror movie. It was very scary.

↓

A: I'm so tired. I didn't sleep last night.
B: ______________________________
A: ______________________________
B: ______________________________
A: ______________________________

Words **take a bus** 버스를 타다 **snowman** 눈사람 **walk one's dog** 개를 산책시키다 **face** 얼굴 **lock** 잠그다 **all night** 밤새도록 **horror movie** 공포 영화 **scary** 무서운

Wrap-Up Test

[1-2] 빈칸에 들어갈 수 없는 것을 고르세요.

1.

She didn't __________ the book.

① buy ② wrote
③ read ④ borrow
⑤ want

2.

Did you ____________________ in the morning?

① brush your teeth
② wash your face
③ went jogging
④ listen to music
⑤ drink lemon juice

3. 빈칸에 알맞은 말이 바르게 짝지어진 것을 고르세요.

A: __________ you go to the library a few days ago?
B: Yes, I __________. I __________ math.

① Do – do – study
② Do – did – studied
③ Did – did – studyed
④ Did – did – studied
⑤ Did – do – studied

[4-5] 빈칸에 알맞은 것을 고르세요.

4.

A: Did he go out last night?
B: ____________________ He stayed at home.

① Yes, he was. ② Yes, he did.
③ No, he doesn't. ④ No, he didn't.
⑤ Yes, he does.

Words: **borrow** 빌리다 **lemon** 레몬 **library** 도서관 **go out** 외출하다 **stay** 머무르다

5.

A: Did you watch the movie last weekend?
B: ________________ It was very interesting.

① Yes, we are. ② Yes, we do.
③ Yes, we did. ④ No, we don't.
⑤ No, we didn't.

6. 부정문으로 바꿀 때 빈칸에 알맞은 것을 고르세요.

She lost the flight ticket.
→ She ____________ the flight ticket.

① don't lose ② doesn't lost
③ didn't lose ④ didn't lost
⑤ doesn't lose

7. 의문문으로 바꿀 때 빈칸에 알맞은 것을 고르세요.

The concert began at 9.
→ ________ the concert ________ at 9?

① Do – began ② Does – begin
③ Did – began ④ Did – begin
⑤ Does – began

8. 빈칸에 공통으로 알맞은 말을 쓰세요.

- She ________ not come to the party last Sunday.
- Linda, ________ they make fun of your name before?

9. 틀린 문장을 고르세요.

① Did they eat out last Friday?
② Did you turn on the light?
③ Did the train leave at 3 o'clock?
④ He didn't play the drums at the festival.
⑤ My mom didn't made cookies in the evening.

Words
weekend 주말 **interesting** 흥미로운 **flight** 비행, 항공편 **make fun of** ~을 놀리다
eat out 외식하다 **turn on** ~을 켜다 **light** 전등 **festival** 축제

10. 우리말을 영어로 바르게 옮긴 것을 고르세요.

Amanda는 어젯밤에 잘 잤니?

① Does Amanda sleep well last night?
② Does Amanda sleeps well last night?
③ Did Amanda sleep well last night?
④ Did Amanda slept well last night?
⑤ Did Amanda sleeps well last night?

11. 올바른 문장을 고르세요.

① I don't live in Tokyo before.
② Did she forgot my address?
③ Mr. Smith didn't have any money now.
④ Does the class start late last Monday?
⑤ Tina didn't do her homework yesterday.

서술형

12. 빈칸에 알맞은 말을 써서 대화를 완성하세요.

A: __________ __________ __________ Peter this morning?
B: No, I didn't. I met Ryan.

서술형

13. 우리말과 같은 뜻이 되도록 주어진 말을 이용하여 문장을 완성하세요.

Kate는 어제 머리를 감지 않았다.
(wash her hair)

→ Kate ______________________________ yesterday.

서술형

14. 틀린 부분을 찾아 바르게 고쳐 쓰세요.

Did the girls took the bus an hour ago?

→ ______________________________
____

서술형

15. 다음 글을 읽고, 질문에 알맞은 답을 쓰세요.

James got up late this morning, so he didn't have breakfast and ran to school.

(1) Did James get up late?
– __________, __________ __________.

(2) Did James have breakfast?
– __________, __________ __________.

Words **Tokyo** (일본) 도쿄 **address** 주소 **start** 시작하다 **hair** 머리카락

UNIT 05

형용사

Vocab Check! 이번 과에서 배울 단어의 뜻을 확인하고, 모르는 단어에 체크 표시하세요.

1	cloud	명 구름	11	little	형 어린	21	difficult	형 어려운
2	prince	명 왕자	12	tasty	형 맛있는	22	voice	명 목소리
3	question	명 문제, 질문	13	place	명 장소	23	sharp	형 날카로운
4	pink	형 분홍색의	14	honest	형 정직한	24	round	형 둥근
5	finger	명 손가락	15	doughnut	명 도넛	25	castle	명 성
6	sweet	형 달콤한	16	lovely	형 사랑스러운	26	comfortable	형 편안한
7	wise	형 현명한	17	god	명 신	27	deep	형 깊은
8	kitchen	명 부엌	18	bridge	명 다리	28	lake	명 호수
9	blond	형 금발의	19	island	명 섬	29	diligent	형 부지런한
10	death	명 죽음	20	empty	형 텅 빈	30	principal	명 교장

UNIT 05 형용사

My uncle has a truck.
나의 삼촌은 트럭을 한 대 가지고 있어요.

It is an old truck. It is very big and heavy.
그것은 낡은 트럭이에요. 그것은 매우 크고 무거워요.

It is not expensive.
그것은 값이 비싸지 않아요.

A 형용사: ~인, ~한

형용사는 명사의 모양이나 상태, 기분 등을 구체적으로 나타내는 말로, '~인,' '~한'이라고 해석해요.

1. 여러 가지 형용사

크기, 모양, 외모	tall ((키가) 큰), big ((크기가) 큰), round (둥근), pretty (예쁜), ugly (못생긴), handsome (잘생긴), fat (뚱뚱한), thin (얇은, 마른), thick (두꺼운)
기분, 성격	good (좋은), happy (행복한), sad (슬픈), kind (친절한), lazy (게으른), angry (화난), honest (정직한), active (활동적인)
상태	new (새로운), young (어린), rich (부유한), cheap (값이 싼), sharp (날카로운)
색깔	white (흰), black (검은), blue (파란), yellow (노란), green (녹색의)
날씨	rainy (비가 오는), windy (바람 부는), sunny (화창한), hot (더운), dry (건조한), warm (따뜻한), cool (시원한), cloudy (흐린), foggy (안개가 낀)

2. 반대 의미의 형용사

good (좋은) ↔ bad (나쁜)	fast (빠른) ↔ slow (느린)	big, large (큰) ↔ small (작은)
high (높은) ↔ low (낮은)	poor (가난한) ↔ rich (부유한)	clean (깨끗한) ↔ dirty (더러운)

cheap (싼) ↔ expensive (비싼)	lazy (게으른) ↔ diligent (부지런한)
hot (뜨거운, 더운) ↔ cold (차가운, 추운)	happy (행복한) ↔ unhappy (불행한)

tall (키가 큰), long (긴) ↔ short (키가 작은 / 짧은)

new (새로운), young (어린) ↔ old (낡은, 오래된 / 나이가 많은)

어떤 형용사는 앞에 un을 붙여서 반대 의미를 나타내기도 해요.

B 형용사 + 명사

형용사는 명사의 앞에 쓰여 명사의 의미를 구체적으로 설명해줘요.

형용사는 뒤에 나오는 명사의 의미를 꾸며줘요.
good news (좋은 소식)

1. 관사(a, an, the) + 형용사 + 명사

a (어떤)	**sunny** (화창한) **good** (좋은) **happy** (행복한)	day (날)

an **old** radio
He is a **rich** man.
There are **tall** trees.
The **dirty** socks are not mine.

2. 소유격(my, her, their 등) + 형용사 + 명사

my (나의)	**new** (새로운) **slow** (느린) **expensive** (비싼)	computer (컴퓨터)

his **cute** baby
I like her **brown** eyes.
That is their **new** house.
Who is your **favorite** singer?

C 주어 + be동사 + 형용사

형용사는 be동사의 뒤에 쓰여 주어를 보충 설명해줘요.

be동사 뒤에는 명사가 올 수도 있어요.
It is a pen.
(그것은 펜이다.)

You (당신은)	are (~이다)	**smart.** (똑똑한) **kind.** (친절한) **handsome.** (잘생긴)

They are **poor.**
She is **kind.**
The sky is **blue.**
The house is **large.**

My Grammar Notes

1 형용사: ____________를 구체적으로 설명하거나 주어를 보충 설명하는 말

2 반대 의미의 형용사: good ↔ __________ clean ↔ __________ __________ ↔ diligent
__________ ↔ short new ↔ __________ __________ ↔ rich

3 형용사의 위치 (1) 명사 앞: (관사/소유격 +)____________ + ____________
(2) be동사 뒤: 주어 + ____________ + 형용사

Warm-Up

A 형용사를 찾아 O 표시하세요. 여러 가지 형용사

lazy	cloud	fat	dry	know
love	young	prince	child	handsome

B 서로 반대 의미의 형용사를 연결하세요. 반대 의미의 형용사

1. poor • • ⓐ new
2. lazy • • ⓑ high
3. short • • ⓒ tall
4. fast • • ⓓ rich
5. old • • ⓔ slow
6. low • • ⓕ diligent

C 형용사에 밑줄을 긋고, 형용사가 설명하는 말에 O 표시하세요.

형용사 + 명사

1. There is a pretty flower.
2. This is my new computer.
3. Jenny has a big bag.
4. The singer has brown hair.
5. That is an old television.
6. Peter gives me sweet doughnuts.

Words

cloud 구름
prince 왕자
flower 꽃
brown 갈색의
hair 머리카락
television 텔레비전
sweet 달콤한
doughnut 도넛

D 우리말과 같은 뜻이 되도록 알맞은 것을 고르세요. 형용사 + 명사

1. 맛있는 주스 → (juice delicious / delicious juice)
2. 키가 큰 소년들 → (boys tall / tall boys)
3. 작은 열쇠 → (a small key / small a key)
4. 그의 하얀 개 → (dog his white / his white dog)
5. 초록색 사과 → (a green apple / green an apple)
6. 그의 금발 머리 → (his blond hair / blond his hair)
7. 나의 새 친구들 → (new my friends / my new friends)
8. 그녀의 멋진 부엌 → (her nice kitchen / nice her kitchen)

Words

juice 주스
key 열쇠
blond 금발의
kitchen 부엌
weather 날씨
fresh 신선한
famous 유명한
smart 영리한

E 우리말과 같은 뜻이 되도록 바르게 연결하세요. 주어 + be동사 + 형용사

1.	그는 유명하다.	He •	• ⓐ are nice.
2.	그들은 친절하다.	They •	• ⓑ are fresh.
3.	네 신발은 멋지다.	Your shoes •	• ⓒ is famous.
4.	그녀의 집은 예쁘다.	Her house •	• ⓓ is blue.
5.	그 달걀들은 신선하다.	The eggs •	• ⓔ is pretty.
6.	그의 모자는 파랗다.	His hat •	• ⓕ are kind.
7.	Jenny는 영리하다.	Jenny •	• ⓖ is cold.
8.	날씨가 춥다.	The weather •	• ⓗ is smart.

Practice

A 빈칸에 알맞지 않은 것을 고르세요.

1.	a ________ dog	☐ brown	☐ cute	✓ mine
2.	my ________ friends	☐ new	☐ love	☐ good
3.	an ________ camera	☐ have	☐ old	☐ expensive
4.	a ________ book	☐ fun	☐ my	☐ famous
5.	your ________ sister	☐ little	☐ are	☐ lazy
6.	a ________ garden	☐ place	☐ nice	☐ beautiful
7.	________ stories	☐ a	☐ sad	☐ short
8.	his ________ house	☐ big	☐ clean	☐ room

Words

little 어린
place 장소
story 이야기 (복수형 **stories**)
tablet 태블릿 PC
honest 정직한
smile 미소
skirt 치마
look good 좋아 보인다

B 주어진 단어를 바르게 배열하여 문장을 완성하세요.

1. This is (white / shirt / my). → This is my white shirt.
2. She is (a / teacher / kind). →
3. It is (his / tablet / old). →
4. He is (honest / an / boy). →
5. (blue / bag / the) is yours. →
6. I love (your / smile / sweet). →
7. It's (song / their / new). →
8. (red / the / skirt) looks good. →

C 우리말과 같은 뜻이 되도록 알맞은 단어를 고른 후, 문장을 완성하세요.

Words

leg 다리
train 기차
mountain 산
cell phone 휴대전화

1. 키가 큰 (tall / short)
   Ben은 키가 크다. → Ben is tall .
2. 깨끗한 (clean / dirty)
   이 컵들은 깨끗하다. → These cups ______ .
3. 행복한 (happy / unhappy)
   그들은 행복하다. → They ______ .
4. 추운 (hot / cold)
   나는 지금 춥다. → I ______ now.
5. 비싼 (cheap / expensive)
   내 차는 비싸다. → My car ______ .
6. 짧은 (long / short)
   그의 다리는 짧다. → His legs ______ .
7. 빠른 (slow / fast)
   이 기차는 빠르다. → This train ______ .
8. 부유한 (rich / poor)
   그 노인은 부유하다. → The old man ______ .
9. 작은 (big / small)
   Alice의 방은 작다. → Alice's room ______ .
10. 높은 (low / high)
    이 산은 높다. → This mountain ______ .
11. 새로운 (new / old)
    내 휴대전화는 새것이다. → My cell phone ______ .

D 두 문장의 의미를 한 문장으로 나타내세요.

1. She is a student. + The student is smart.
→ She is a smart student.

2. He has a rabbit. + The rabbit is brown.
→

3. Bob made a sandwich. + His sandwich was tasty.
→

4. There is a table. + The table is round.
→

5. We visited a building. + The building was tall.
→

6. It is a balloon. + The balloon is big.
→

7. Sophia read books. + The books were interesting.
→

8. Jennifer is an actress. + She is beautiful.
→

9. This is a castle. + The castle is old.
→

10. I have shoes. + The shoes are comfortable.
→

Words

sandwich 샌드위치
tasty 맛있는
round 둥근
balloon 풍선
interesting 흥미로운
actress (여자) 배우
castle 성
comfortable 편안한

E 두 문장의 의미가 통하도록 빈칸에 알맞은 말을 쓰세요.

1. He is a wise man. → The man is wise.
2. It is an easy question. → The question ________.
3. It is a beautiful island. → The island ________.
4. It is a wonderful picture. → The picture ________.
5. It was a difficult test. → The test ________.
6. This is an empty box. → This box ________.
7. It is a hot stove. → The stove ________.
8. It is an exciting game. → The game ________.
9. They were yellow leaves. → The leaves ________.

F 밑줄 친 부분을 바르게 고쳐 쓰세요.

1. My brother is kind a boy. → ________
2. These TVs are an cheap. → ________
3. Your jacket black looks nice. → ________
4. These are pink my socks. → ________
5. I like her voice lovely. → ________
6. We new house is large. → ________
7. The weather cloudy is. → ________
8. The woman old is my grandma. → ________

Words

wise 현명한
easy 쉬운
question 문제, 질문
island 섬
wonderful 멋진
picture 그림, 사진
difficult 어려운
test 시험
empty 텅 빈
stove 난로
exciting 신나는
leaf 나뭇잎 (복수형 **leaves**)
pink 분홍색의
voice 목소리
lovely 사랑스러운
cloudy (날씨가) 흐린
grandma 할머니

Grammar into Writing

A 우리말과 같은 뜻이 되도록 주어진 말을 바르게 배열하세요.

1. 이 영화는 지루하다. this movie / boring / is

→ This movie is boring.

2. 내 고양이들은 뚱뚱했다. were / my cats / fat

→ ______________________

3. 그 수학 문제는 어렵다. is / difficult / the math question

→ ______________________

4. 그녀의 손가락은 길다. long / are / her fingers

→ ______________________

5. 저 호수는 깊었다. that lake / was / deep

→ ______________________

6. 컴퓨터 게임은 재미있다. computer games / fun / are

→ ______________________

B 우리말과 같은 뜻이 되도록 주어진 말을 이용하여 영작하세요.

1. green / coat / warm

1) 너의 초록색 코트 → your green coat

2) 너의 초록색 코트는 따뜻하다. → Your green coat is warm.

2. smart / boy / short

1) 그 키가 작은 소년 → the __________ __________

2) 그 키가 작은 소년은 영리하다. → ______________________

3. laptop / new / expensive

1) 나의 새 노트북 → my ______ ______

2) 나의 새 노트북은 비싸다. → ____________________

4. old / car / dirty

1) 그 오래된 차 → the ______ ______

2) 그 오래된 차는 더럽다. → ____________________

5. handsome / prince / lazy

1) 그 잘생긴 왕자 → the ______ ______

2) 그 잘생긴 왕자는 게으르다. → ____________________

C 다음 글을 읽고 그림과 일치하지 않는 부분에 표시한 다음, 고쳐서 다시 써보세요.

I am Cerberus. I have two heads. But I have three bodies. My faces and body are scary. My teeth are sharp. My body is yellow. My tail is short. My master is Hades. He is the god of death.

↓

I am Cerberus. ____________________

____

____

Words
boring 지루한 **finger** 손가락 **lake** 호수 **deep** 깊은 **Cerberus** 케르베로스 (저승 세계를 지키는 괴물) **head** 머리 **body** 몸 **scary** 무서운 **sharp** 날카로운 **tail** 꼬리 **master** 주인 **Hades** 하데스 (죽음의 신) **god** 신 **death** 죽음

Wrap-Up Test

1. 형용사가 아닌 것을 고르세요.

① heart ② angry
③ sunny ④ fast
⑤ new

2. 반의어 관계가 아닌 것을 고르세요.

① high – low
② fast – slow
③ poor – kind
④ old – young
⑤ happy – unhappy

3. 다음 문장에서 short가 들어갈 위치를 고르세요.

① The rabbit ② has ③ a ④ tail ⑤.

[4-5] 빈칸에 들어갈 수 없는 것을 고르세요.

4.

The woman is ________.

① lovely ② like
③ brave ④ funny
⑤ a designer

5.

You are a ________ soccer player.

① great ② popular
③ handsome ④ world
⑤ smart

Words **angry** 화가 난 **brave** 용감한 **soccer player** 축구선수 **popular** 인기 있는

[6-7] 빈칸에 알맞은 것을 고르세요.

6.

The bridge ______________.
(저 다리는 길다.)

① long ② tall
③ is long ④ is tall
⑤ is a long

7.

Her pink dress is ______________.

① expensive ② look
③ the girl ④ a beautiful
⑤ the large

8. 두 문장이 같은 의미가 되도록 빈칸에 알맞은 말을 쓰세요.

These are difficult questions.
= These questions ______________
______________.

9. 밑줄 친 부분의 의미가 다른 것을 고르세요.

① Her watch is old.
② I have an old radio.
③ My father's car is old.
④ There are old buildings.
⑤ The old man is our principal.

10. 틀린 문장을 고르세요.

① Steve is a famous actor.
② My sister and I are tired.
③ The dancer has hair blue.
④ The dirty shoes are mine.
⑤ Those are his new neighbors.

Words **bridge** 다리 **principal** 교장 **tired** 피곤한 **dancer** 무용수, 댄서 **neighbor** 이웃

서술형

11. 올바른 문장을 고르세요.

① Jane is a pretty.

② He is an honest man.

③ Kind woman is my aunt.

④ Cheetahs are animals fast.

⑤ There are a small oranges in the basket.

12. 우리말을 영어로 바르게 옮긴 것을 고르세요.

Jessica는 내가 가장 좋아하는 가수이다.

① Jessica is my singer favorite.

② Jessica is favorite singer my.

③ Jessica is my favorite singer.

④ Jessica is singer my favorite.

⑤ Jessica is favorite my singer.

서술형

13. 두 문장의 의미를 한 문장으로 나타내세요.

Sue is a student. The student is diligent.

→ Sue is ___________ ___________

___________.

서술형

14. 틀린 부분을 찾아 바르게 고쳐 쓰세요.

A hippo has big a mouth.

→ ______________________________

____

서술형

15. 우리말과 같은 뜻이 되도록 주어진 말을 바르게 배열하세요.

수영은 좋은 스포츠이다.

(is / sport / good / a)

→ Swimming ______________________

______________________________.

Words
cheetah 치타 **animal** 동물 **basket** 바구니 **favorite** 가장 좋아하는
hippo 하마 **sport** 스포츠, 운동 (경기)

UNIT 06

지시형용사
수량형용사

Vocab Check! 이번 과에서 배울 단어의 뜻을 확인하고, 모르는 단어에 체크 표시하세요.

1	cheap	형 (값이) 싼	11	deer	명 사슴	21	goldfish	명 금붕어
2	painting	명 그림	12	visit	동 방문하다	22	sausage	명 소시지
3	town	명 마을	13	witch	명 마녀	23	vase	명 꽃병
4	cousin	명 사촌	14	bottle	명 병	24	pond	명 연못
5	backpack	명 배낭	15	balloon	명 풍선	25	fry	동 굽다, 튀기다
6	delicious	형 맛있는	16	look good on	~에게 잘 어울리다	26	sheep	명 양
7	salt	명 소금	17	meal	명 식사	27	spoon	명 숟가락
8	fork	명 포크	18	country	명 나라	28	sand	명 모래
9	novel	명 소설	19	smell	동 냄새가 나다	29	coin	명 동전
10	oil	명 석유, 기름	20	fresh	형 신선한	30	cage	명 새장

UNIT 06

지시형용사, 수량형용사

This box is big.
이 상자는 커요.

There are many toys in the box.
상자 안에는 많은 장난감들이 있어요.

There are a few dolls, too.
인형 몇 개도 있어요.

A this, that, these, those: 이 ~, 저 ~

this, that, these, those는 대명사로 쓰일 뿐만 아니라 명사 앞에 쓰여 명사를 꾸며줄 수도 있어요. 이때는 형용사와 같은 역할을 하므로 지시형용사라고 해요.

this (이 ~)	단수명사, 셀 수 없는 명사	**this** book (이 책)	**this** milk (이 우유)
that (저 ~)		**that** book (저 책)	**that** milk (저 우유)
these (이 ~들)	복수명사	**these** books (이 책들)	**these** desks (이 책상들)
those (저 ~들)		**those** books (저 책들)	**those** desks (저 책상들)

This bag is heavy. (이 가방은 무거워요.)
That boy is kind. (저 소년은 친절해요.)
These apples are fresh. (이 사과들은 신선해요.)
Those people are Italians. (저 사람들은 이탈리아 사람들이에요.)

Mini Grammar 참고 1권 Unit 04

지시대명사 *vs.* 지시형용사

지시대명사는 '이것(들), 저것(들)'이라는 의미이지만, 지시형용사는 명사와 함께 쓰여 '이 ~, 저 ~'의 의미를 나타내요.

This is my computer. (이것은 나의 컴퓨터이다.)
지시대명사

This **computer** is mine. (이 컴퓨터는 나의 것이다.)
지시형용사

B many, much, a lot of: 많은

many는 수가 많음을, much는 양이 많음을 나타내고, a lot of는 두 가지 경우에 모두 쓸 수 있어요.

many	셀 수 있는 명사
much	셀 수 없는 명사
a lot of	둘 다 가능

many pens (많은 펜들) ⇔ **a lot of** pens

much water (많은 물) ⇔ **a lot of** water

a lot of는 lots of, plenty of로도 쓸 수 있어요.

Mike is making **many[a lot of] cookies**.

I don't drink **much[a lot of] coffee**.

C a few, a little: 약간의, 조금의 / few, little: 거의 없는

(a) few는 명사의 앞에서 '수'를 나타내고, (a) little은 '양'을 나타내는 수량형용사예요.

긍정	**a few**	bags	복수명사	가방이 조금 있는
	a little	rain	셀 수 없는 명사	비가 조금 오는
부정	**few**	bags	복수명사	가방이 거의 없는
	little	rain	셀 수 없는 명사	비가 거의 안 오는

There are **a few flowers** in the vase. (긍정)

There are **few flowers** in the vase. (부정)

We have **a little time**. (긍정)

We have **little time**. (부정)

few와 little은 단어 자체에 이미 부정의 의미가 있어서 문장에 not을 쓸 필요가 없어요.

My Grammar Notes

1 지시형용사: this, ____________, ____________, ____________ + 명사

this / that + ____________명사, ____________ / ____________ + 복수명사

2 many[a lot of] + 복수명사, much[a lot of] + 셀 수 없는 명사

____________ songs = a lot of songs ____________ love = a lot of love

3 a few와 few는 '수'를, a little과 little은 '양'을 나타낼 때 쓴다.

a few / ____________ people ____________ / little water

Warm-Up

A 지시형용사에는 O, 지시대명사에는 ㅁ 표시하세요.

this, that, these, those

1. This juice is cool.
2. This is my old bicycle.
3. That is my uncle John.
4. That lady is my mother.
5. Those babies smile a lot.
6. Those are not my T-shirts.
7. These are my best friends.
8. These computers are brand-new.

B ( ) 안에서 알맞은 것을 고르세요.

this, that, these, those

1. 이 열쇠 → (this key / that key)
2. 저 장난감들 → (these toys / those toys)
3. 저 도서관 → (this library / that library)
4. 이 뜨거운 차 → (this hot tea / that hot tea)
5. 이 컵케이크들 → (this cupcake / these cupcakes)
6. 이 오렌지들 → (these oranges / those oranges)
7. 저 예쁜 정원 → (that pretty garden / those pretty gardens)
8. 저 귀여운 토끼들 → (that cute rabbit / those cute rabbits)

Words

cool 차가운
bicycle 자전거
smile 미소 짓다
a lot 많이
brand-new 최신의
library 도서관
hot 뜨거운
tea 차
cupcake 컵케이크
garden 정원
cute 귀여운
rabbit 토끼

C 우리말과 같은 뜻이 되도록 알맞은 것을 고르세요.

many, much, a lot of

1. 많은 트럭 → (many / much) trucks
2. 많은 우유 → (many / much) milk
3. 많은 숟가락 → (many / much) spoons
4. 많은 나무 → (much / a lot of) trees
5. 많은 돈 → (many / a lot of) money
6. 많은 양 → (many / much) sheep
7. 많은 모래 → (many / much) sand
8. 많은 자동차 → (a lot of / much) cars

Words

truck 트럭
spoon 숟가락
sheep 양 (복수형 **sheep**)
sand 모래
coin 동전
sugar 설탕

D 우리말과 같은 뜻이 되도록 알맞은 말을 보기에서 골라 쓰세요.

(a) few, (a) little

보기 few a few little a little

1. 버터가 조금 있는 → a little butter
2. 꽃이 조금 있는 → ______ flowers
3. 책이 거의 없는 → ______ books
4. 물이 조금 있는 → ______ water
5. 우유가 거의 없는 → ______ milk
6. 동전이 거의 없는 → ______ coins
7. 달걀이 조금 있는 → ______ eggs
8. 설탕이 조금 있는 → ______ sugar

Practice

A ( ) 안에서 알맞은 것을 고르세요.

1. (This / These) cake is delicious.
2. (This / These) clothes are warm.
3. (This / These) puppy is cute.
4. (This / These) roses are beautiful.
5. (That / Those) cookies are mine.
6. (That / Those) sausage is big.
7. (That / Those) tomatoes are fresh.
8. (This / These) boy is my little brother.

B ( ) 안에서 알맞은 것을 모두 고르세요.

1. The girl has (many / much) dolls.
2. I have (many / much) comic books.
3. There isn't (many / much) air in the plane.
4. There are (many / much) forks on the table.
5. Mia reads (many / much / a lot of) novels these days.
6. There isn't (many / much / a lot of) water in the country.
7. Josh usually puts (many / much / a lot of) salt in his food.
8. Taylor Swift has (many / much / a lot of) fans around the world.

Words

delicious 맛있는
clothes 옷
warm 따뜻한
rose 장미
sausage 소시지
fresh 신선한
doll 인형
comic book 만화책
air 공기
plane 비행기
fork 포크
novel 소설
country 나라
salt 소금
fan 팬
around the world 전 세계에

C 우리말과 같은 뜻이 되도록 알맞은 것을 고르세요.

1. 나는 돈이 거의 없다.

→ I have (few / little) money.

2. Bill은 친구가 거의 없다.

→ Bill has (few / a few) friends.

3. 우리는 치즈를 조금 가지고 있다.

→ We have (little / a little) cheese.

4. 유나는 자유시간이 거의 없다.

→ Yuna has (few / little) free time.

5. 나는 식사 후에 차를 조금 마신다.

→ I drink (a few / a little) tea after a meal.

6. 하늘에 구름이 거의 없다.

→ There are (few / a few) clouds in the sky.

7. 새장에 몇 마리의 새가 있었다.

→ There were (few / a few) birds in the cage.

8. 연못에 금붕어가 거의 없다.

→ There are (few / little) goldfish in the pond.

9. 꽃병에 장미가 몇 송이 있다.

→ There are (a few / a little) roses in the vase.

10. 수진이는 청바지를 몇 벌 가지고 있다.

→ Sujin has (a few / a little) pairs of blue jeans.

11. 그 서점에는 잡지가 거의 없었다.

→ There were (few / little) magazines at the bookstore.

12. 놀이공원에 사람이 거의 없다.

→ There are (few / little) people in the amusement park.

Words

free time 자유시간
meal 식사
sky 하늘
cage 새장
goldfish 금붕어
pond 연못
vase 꽃병
blue jeans 청바지
magazine 잡지
bookstore 서점
amusement park 놀이공원

D 우리말과 같은 뜻이 되도록 this, that, these, those 중 알맞은 것을 쓰세요.

1. 이 모자는 내 생일 선물이다.
→ This cap is my birthday present.

2. 저 가수는 노래를 아주 잘한다.
→ ______ singer sings very well.

3. 이 아이들은 Emily의 사촌들이다.
→ ______ children are Emily's cousins.

4. 저 풍선들은 우리의 파티를 위한 것이다.
→ ______ balloons are for our party.

5. 저 돌고래는 높이 뛴다.
→ ______ dolphin jumps high.

6. 이 사슴들은 긴 다리를 가지고 있다.
→ ______ deer have long legs.

7. 이 비누는 향이 좋다.
→ ______ soap smells good.

8. 저 바나나들은 맛있게 보인다.
→ ______ bananas look delicious.

9. 저 손목시계는 너무 비싸다.
→ ______ watch is too expensive.

10. 이 드레스는 너에게 잘 어울린다.
→ ______ dress looks good on you.

11. 저 사람들은 나의 이웃들이었다.
→ ______ people were my neighbors.

Words

cap 모자
present 선물
cousin 사촌
balloon 풍선
dolphin 돌고래
deer 사슴 (복수형 **deer**)
soap 비누
smell 냄새가 나다
watch 손목시계
look good on ~에게 잘 어울리다
neighbor 이웃

E 우리말과 같은 뜻이 되도록 보기에서 알맞은 말을 골라 문장을 완성하세요.

보기 many much a few few a little little

1. 설탕이 거의 없다. (sugar)
→ There is little sugar.

2. 그녀는 돈이 조금 있었다. (money)
→ She had ______.

3. Emma는 좋은 친구가 많다. (good friend)
→ Emma has ______.

4. 나는 집에 몇 마리의 귀여운 개가 있다. (cute dog)
→ I have ______ in my house.

5. 정원에는 나무가 거의 없다. (tree)
→ There are ______ in the garden.

6. Tim은 그 양파를 약간의 버터에 볶았다. (butter)
→ Tim fried the onions in ______.

7. 병에는 오렌지 주스가 많지 않다. (orange juice)
→ There isn't ______ in the bottle.

8. 내 할아버지는 몇 개의 오래된 라디오를 가지고 있다. (old radio)
→ My grandfather has ______.

9. 이 동굴에는 빛이 거의 없다. (light)
→ There is ______ in this cave.

10. 몇 마리의 자이언트 판다가 중국에 살았다. (giant panda)
→ ______ lived in China.

Words

fry (기름에) 굽다, 튀기다
onion 양파
bottle 병
radio 라디오
light 전등; 빛
cave 동굴
giant panda 자이언트 판다 (털이 흰색과 검은색인 중국산 희귀동물)

Grammar into Writing

A 우리말과 같은 뜻이 되도록 주어진 말을 바르게 배열하세요.

1. 이 컴퓨터들은 최신형이다. are / computers / brand-new / these

→ These computers are brand-new.

2. 나는 몇 개의 배낭을 가지고 있다. have / I / a few / backpacks

→ ______

3. 나는 많은 음악을 내려받았다. a lot of / downloaded / I / music

→ ______

4. 그 로켓에는 공기가 거의 없다. is / there / in the rocket / little / air

→ ______

5. 그 도서관에는 많은 책이 있다. there / in the library / many / are / books

→ ______

B 우리말과 같은 뜻이 되도록 주어진 말을 이용하여 문장을 완성하세요.

1. 1) 이 소년들은 내 남동생들이다.

→ These boys are my brothers.

2) 저 가수들은 유명하다. (singer, famous)

→ Those singers are famous.

2. 1) 겨울에 눈이 많이 오지 않는다.

→ We don't have ______ snow in winter.

2) 여름에 비가 많이 오지 않는다. (rain, in summer)

→ ______

3. 1) 그는 많은 친구들이 있다.

→ He has ____________ friends.

2) 그녀는 많은 만화책을 가지고 있다. (comic book)

→ ____

4. 1) 나의 돼지 저금통에는 동전이 조금 있다.

→ There are ____________ coins in my piggy bank.

2) 접시에 소스가 약간 있다. (sauce, on the plate)

→ ____

5. 1) 사막에는 물이 거의 없다.

→ There is ____________ water in the desert.

2) 하늘에 별이 거의 없다. (star, in the sky)

→ ____

C 다음 글을 읽고 틀린 부분을 찾아 표시한 다음, 고쳐서 다시 써보세요.

The witch visits Snow White's house. In the witch's basket, there are much apples. That apples look delicious. Snow White likes apples. But she has few money.

↓

The witch visits ____

____

____

Words

backpack 배낭 **download** 다운로드하다, 내려받다 **rocket** 로켓 **piggy bank** 돼지 저금통 **sauce** 소스, 양념 **plate** 접시 **desert** 사막 **witch** 마녀 **visit** 방문하다 **Snow White** 백설공주 **basket** 바구니

Wrap-Up Test

1. 영어와 우리말이 잘못 짝지어진 것을 고르세요.

① a lot of - 많은
② a few - 조금 있는
③ few - 거의 없는
④ much - 많은
⑤ a little - 거의 없는

2. 밑줄 친 부분의 의미가 다른 것을 고르세요.

① This is his umbrella.
② This notebook is hers.
③ This pizza is delicious.
④ They live in this house.
⑤ I like this painting very much.

3. 빈칸에 알맞은 말을 고르세요.

I don't have __________ money.

① many
② much
③ a few
④ few
⑤ these

4. 빈칸에 알맞은 말을 모두 고르세요. (2개)

Yuna Kim has ______________ fans in Korea.

① much
② many
③ a lot of
④ a little
⑤ little

5. 빈칸에 공통으로 알맞은 것을 고르세요.

- __________ is my new camera.
- __________ dog has long ears.

① This
② These
③ Many
④ Few
⑤ Little

Words umbrella 우산 notebook 공책 painting 그림 camera 카메라

6. 빈칸에 알맞은 말이 바르게 짝지어진 것을 고르세요.

- Kate has __________ friends.
- I drink __________ milk every morning.

① little – a little ② few – a few
③ a little – a few ④ a few – a little
⑤ little – a few

7. 빈칸에 들어갈 수 없는 것을 고르세요.

There are ______________ books in the bookstore.

① a few ② many
③ a little ④ a lot of
⑤ plenty of

8. 밑줄 친 부분이 어색한 것을 고르세요.

① These coat is too big.
② That boy is my cousin.
③ We have a lot of cheese.
④ My sister has a few watches.
⑤ Leo has little money in his wallet.

9. 우리말을 영어로 바르게 옮긴 것을 고르세요.

시간이 거의 없다.

① There is few time.
② There is a little time.
③ There is little time.
④ There is not little time.
⑤ There is not a few time.

10. 빈칸에 many를 쓸 수 없는 것을 고르세요.

① The store has _______ flowers.
② She has _______ dolls in her room.
③ We saw _______ monkeys in the zoo.
④ There are _______ people in the bank.
⑤ I drink _______ orange juice every day.

Words **coat** 코트 **watch** 손목시계 **wallet** 지갑 **store** 상점, 가게 **monkey** 원숭이 **bank** 은행

11. 틀린 문장을 고르세요.

① Those caps are cheap.

② My car uses a lot of oil.

③ There are many stars in the sky.

④ There are a little trees in the town.

⑤ This woman is my swimming coach.

[12-13] 우리말과 같은 뜻이 되도록 빈칸에 알맞은 말을 쓰세요.

서술형

12.

I need ______________ help.
(나는 약간의 도움이 필요하다.)

서술형

13.

There are ______________ buses in this town.
(이 마을에는 버스가 거의 없다.)

서술형

14. 틀린 부분을 찾아 바르게 고쳐 쓰세요.

This red roses are very fresh.

______________ → ______________

서술형

15. 우리말과 같은 뜻이 되도록 주어진 말을 바르게 배열하세요.

제주도에는 많은 말들이 있다.
(lot / there / a / of / horses / are)

→ ______________________________
on Jeju Island.

Words **cheap** (가격이) 싼 **use** 사용하다 **oil** 기름, 석유 **town** 마을 **coach** 코치, 감독 **help** 돕다; 도움 **horse** 말

UNIT 07

who
what

Vocab Check! 이번 과에서 배울 단어의 뜻을 확인하고, 모르는 단어에 체크 표시하세요.

	No.	Word	Meaning		No.	Word	Meaning		No.	Word	Meaning
☑	1	subject	명 과목	☐	11	find	동 발견하다	☐	21	gentleman	명 신사
☐	2	awesome	형 굉장한	☐	12	choose	동 고르다, 선택하다	☐	22	close	형 가까운; 친한
☐	3	month	명 월, 달	☐	13	meet	동 만나다	☐	23	dentist	명 치과 의사
☐	4	remember	동 기억하다	☐	14	son	명 아들	☐	24	twin	형 쌍둥이의
☐	5	move	동 옮기다, 이사하다	☐	15	pencil	명 연필	☐	25	wish	명 소망
☐	6	respect	동 존경하다	☐	16	cross	동 건너다	☐	26	drive	동 운전하다
☐	7	number	명 숫자	☐	17	ballet	명 발레	☐	27	really	부 정말로
☐	8	goal	명 목표	☐	18	shape	명 모양	☐	28	dream	명 꿈
☐	9	marry	동 결혼하다	☐	19	holiday	명 휴일	☐	29	kind	형 친절한 명 종류
☐	10	solve	동 풀다, 해결하다	☐	20	season	명 계절	☐	30	blanket	명 담요

UNIT 07 who, what

What sport **do you like**? – We like **soccer**.
당신들은 무슨 스포츠를 좋아하나요? – 우리는 축구를 좋아해요.

Who **is your favorite player**? – **Messi**.
당신들이 가장 좋아하는 선수는 누구인가요? – 메시예요.

Whose **uniform are these**? – They're **ours**.
이것들은 누구의 유니폼인가요? – 우리들 것이에요.

A 의문사의 종류와 어순

의문사는 정보를 구하는 의문문을 만들 때 사용하는 말로, 문장의 맨 앞에 위치해요.
'누가, 언제, 어디서, 무엇을, 어떻게, 왜'에 관한 정보를 물어볼 수 있어요.

who	when	where	what	how	why
누가	언제	어디서	무엇, 어떤	어떻게	왜

1. be동사를 이용한 의문사 의문문

주어와 be동사의 위치를 바꾸어 의문문을 만들어요.

의문사	be동사	주어 ~?	
Who	are	they?	그들은 누구인가요?
When	is	your birthday?	당신의 생일은 언제인가요?

2. 일반동사를 이용한 의문사 의문문

일반동사가 현재형이면 주어 앞에 do[does]를 쓰고, 과거형이면 주어 앞에 did를 써요.

의문사	do/does/did	주어 + 동사원형 ~?	
What	do	you like?	당신은 무엇을 좋아하나요?
Where	did	he live?	그는 어디에 살았나요?

Mini Grammar

의문사가 없는 의문문 *vs.* 의문사가 있는 의문문

Are you hungry? (당신은 배고픈가요?) + **Why** (왜) ⇨ **Why** are you hungry? (당신은 왜 배고픈가요?)

Did you call me? (당신은 내게 전화했나요?) + **When** (언제) ⇨ **When** did you call me? (당신은 언제 내게 전화했나요?)

B who, whom, whose

사람에 대한 정보를 물을 때는 who, whom, whose를 사용해요.

> 의문사가 주어의 역할을 할 때는 3인칭 단수로 취급해요.

Who (누구, 누가)		is	the boy?	그 소년은 누구인가요?
		helps	you?	누가 당신을 돕나요?
Who, Whom (누구를, 누구에게)		did	you call?	당신은 누구에게 전화했나요?
Whose (누구의)	book (책)	is	that?	저것은 누구의 책인가요?

Who wants more cake?

Whom[Who] do you like most?

Whose house is it?

> 1. whose + 명사: 누구의 ~
> 2. what + 명사: 무슨, 어떤 ~

C what

what은 사물에 대한 정보를 물을 때 사용해요.

What (무엇, 어떤)		is	this?	이것은 무엇인가요?
		do	you want?	당신은 무엇을 원하나요?
What (무슨, 어떤)	color (색)	does	she like?	그녀는 어떤 색깔을 좋아하나요?

What is your blood type?

What does he do?

What time is it now?

What dessert do you like?

My Grammar Notes

1 의문사: __________(누가), __________(언제), where(어디서), __________(무엇을), __________(어떻게), why(왜) 등이 있다.

2 의문사를 이용한 의문문 만들기
(1) 의문사 + __________ + 주어 ~? (2) __________ + do/does/did + 주어 + __________~?

3 __________: 누구, 누가, __________: 누구를, __________ + 명사: 누구의 ~

4 __________: 무엇, 어떤 what + __________: 무슨 ~, 어떤 ~

Warm-Up

A 우리말에 맞는 의문사를 연결하세요. 의문사

1. 누가 •		• ⓐ what
2. 누구의 •		• ⓑ who
3. 무엇을 •		• ⓒ whose
4. 언제 •		• ⓓ how
5. 어디서 •		• ⓔ where
6. 어떻게 •		• ⓕ when
7. 왜 •		• ⓖ why

Words

son 아들
remember 기억하다
best 최고의; 가장
move 옮기다, 이사하다

B ( ) 안에서 알맞은 것을 고르세요. 의문사를 이용한 의문문

1. What (is / does) your name?
2. Why (are / do) you love me?
3. Whose son (is / does) the boy?
4. When (is / does) your birthday?
5. Whom (is / does) he remember?
6. What sport (are / do) you like best?
7. Who (was / did) your English teacher?
8. When did you (move / moved) to Busan?
9. Where (was / did) you buy this computer?

C ( ) 안에서 알맞은 것을 고르세요. who, what

1. (Who / Whose) bag is this?
2. (Whom / Whose) idea is it?
3. (Who / What) is your dream?
4. (What / Whose) color is your car?
5. (Who / Whom) broke the window?
6. (Who / Whose) is that man over there?
7. (Whose / Whom) do you want to meet?
8. (What / Whom) did you call yesterday?
9. (What / Whom) did you do last weekend?
10. (What / Whom) kind of books do you like?

Words

idea 생각, 발상
dream 꿈
break 부수다, 깨뜨리다 (과거형 **broke**)
kind 종류
clothes 옷
invite 초대하다
blue jeans 청바지

D 질문에 알맞은 대답을 연결하세요. who, what

1. Who is she? •	• ⓐ I love my parents.
2. Whose doll is this? •	• ⓑ He is a teacher.
3. Whom do you love? •	• ⓒ She is my sister.
4. What does your father do? •	• ⓓ It's mine.
5. What clothes do you like? •	• ⓔ I want some pizza.
6. Whom did he invite? •	• ⓕ He invited Amy.
7. What do you want for dinner? •	• ⓖ I like blue jeans.

Practice

A 밑줄 친 의문사가 같은 의미로 쓰인 것끼리 연결하세요.

1. What is that? •	• ⓐ Who invited you?
2. Whose pencil is this? •	• ⓑ What is your goal?
3. Who did she ask? •	• ⓒ Whom do you see?
4. Who is singing? •	• ⓓ Whose phone is that?
5. What color is the dress? •	• ⓔ What number did you choose?

Words

pencil 연필
goal 목표
number 숫자
choose 고르다, 선택하다
wish 소망
drive 운전하다
really 정말로
most 가장, 제일
blanket 담요
find 발견하다 (과거형 **found**)

B ( ) 안에서 알맞은 것을 고르세요.

1. Who (is / are) they?
2. What (is / are) your wish?
3. What (am / do) I have to do?
4. Who (drive / drives) the bus?
5. Who (do / does) he really like?
6. What class (do / are) you like most?
7. Who (want / wants) that black blanket?
8. What did you (find / found) in the room?
9. Whom did Peter (visit / visits) yesterday?
10. Who did you (meet / met) in the park yesterday?

C ( ) 안에서 알맞은 것을 고르세요.

1. (Who / Whose / What) is her name?
2. (Who / Whose / Whom) pen is this?
3. (What / Whose / Whom) will you marry?
4. (Who / Whose / Whom) is your best friend?
5. (Who / What / Whom) did you eat for lunch?
6. (Who / Whose / What) gave you this money?
7. (Who / Whose / What) month is your birthday in?

Words

marry 결혼하다
month 월, 달
science 과학
favorite 가장 좋아하는
respect 존경하다
beach 해변

D 보기에서 알맞은 의문사를 모두 골라 쓰세요.

보기 Who Whose Whom What

1. A: What is he studying now?
   B: He is studying science.
2. A: ______ sport do you like?
   B: I like soccer.
3. A: ______ is your favorite singer?
   B: I like Adele.
4. A: ______ notebook is this?
   B: It's Michael's.
5. A: ______ do you respect?
   B: I respect Steve Jobs.
6. A: ______ did you do last weekend?
   B: I went to the beach with my friends.

E 밑줄 친 부분을 바르게 고쳐 쓰세요.

1. What is your ballet teacher? → Who
2. What does he likes to eat? →
3. Who doughnuts are they? →
4. Whose did you call last night? →
5. What subject is you like best? →
6. Whom wrote this book? →
7. What time will you met Nicole? →
8. Who do the girl seeing now? →
9. What did he said to you? →

Words

ballet 발레
doughnut 도넛
subject 과목
write 쓰다 (과거형 **wrote**)
look for ~을 찾다
solve 풀다, 해결하다
animal 동물
stage 무대

F 틀린 부분을 바르게 고쳐 다시 쓰세요.

1. Whose car this is? → Whose car is this?
2. What you are looking for? →
3. Whose bicycle it is? →
4. What did he gave to her? →
5. Whom can solve the problem? →
6. Who did eat my ice cream? →
7. What animal do she likes? →
8. Who are dancing on the stage? →

G 빈칸에 알맞은 의문사를 써서 밑줄 친 부분을 묻는 의문문을 완성하세요.

1. Yuri is playing the violin. → Who is playing the violin?
2. Yuri is playing the violin. → ______ is Yuri playing?
3. Mr. Wilson helped us. → ______ helped us?
4. Mr. Wilson helped us. → ______ did Mr. Wilson help?
5. I broke the cup. → ______ broke the cup?
6. John broke the cup. → ______ did John break?
7. This is Mary's present. → ______ present is this?
8. I enjoy computer games. → ______ do you enjoy?
9. It is my diary. → ______ diary is it?
10. They bought some food. → ______ did they buy?
11. I like tennis. → ______ sport do you like?
12. His car is black. → ______ color is his car?
13. He loves his fans. → ______ does he love?
14. Mrs. Park is my dentist. → ______ is my dentist?
15. My aunt drives a bus. → ______ does your aunt drive?
16. They are Mia's twin brothers.
→ ______ twin brothers are they?
17. Mike is watching a soccer game.
→ ______ is Mike watching?

Words

present 선물
enjoy 즐기다
diary 일기장
fan 팬
dentist 치과 의사
twin 쌍둥이의

Grammar into Writing

A 우리말과 같은 뜻이 되도록 주어진 말을 바르게 배열하세요.

1. 당신이 가장 좋아하는 계절은 무엇인가요? what / favorite season / your / is

→ What is your favorite season?

2. 누가 그 경기에서 이겼나요? won / the match / who

→ ____________________

3. 이것은 누구의 신발인가요? are / shoes / whose / these

→ ____________________

4. 당신은 어떤 과목을 싫어하나요? what / do / you / subject / hate

→ ____________________

5. 그분들은 점심으로 무엇을 드셨나요? they / what / did / for lunch / eat

→ ____________________

B 우리말과 같은 뜻이 되도록 주어진 말을 이용하여 문장을 완성하세요.

1. 1) 누가 영어를 가르치나요?

→ Who teaches English?

2) 누가 일본어를 가르치나요? (Japanese)

→ Who teaches Japanese?

2. 1) 그녀는 누구를 좋아했나요?

→ ________ did she like?

2) 그 영화배우는 누구와 결혼했나요? (the actress, marry)

→ ____________________

3. 1) 당신의 휴대전화는 무슨 색인가요?

→ __________ color is your cell phone?

2) 그녀의 머리카락은 무슨 색인가요? (hair)

→ ______________________________________

4. 1) 이것은 누구의 일기장인가요?

→ __________ diary is this?

2) 이것은 누구의 안경인가요? (glasses)

→ ______________________________________

5. 1) 당신은 어린이날 선물로 무엇을 원하나요?

→ __________ do you want for Children's Day?

2) 당신은 핼러윈에 무엇을 입나요? (wear, on Halloween)

→ ______________________________________

C 빈칸에 알맞은 의문사를 넣어 대화를 완성하세요.

A: Ted, ___whose___ laptop is this?

B: It's mine.

A: It looks great! ____________ gave it to you?

B: My parents bought it for me last week.

A: Awesome! ____________ do you do with it?

B: I do homework and chat with my friends.

Words **season** 계절 **match** 경기 **actress** (여자) 배우 **Halloween** 핼러윈 **awesome** 굉장한

Wrap-Up Test

1. 의문사가 아닌 것을 고르세요.

① who ② whose
③ what ④ that
⑤ when

[2-4] 빈칸에 알맞은 말을 고르세요.

2.

________ season do you like?

① Who ② Whom
③ Whose ④ What
⑤ When

3.

________ gave you this key?

① Who ② Whom
③ Whose ④ What
⑤ Where

4.

________ computer is this?

① Who ② Whom
③ Whose ④ What
⑤ Why

5. 빈칸에 들어갈 말이 나머지와 다른 것을 고르세요.

① ________ birthday is it?
② ________ can I do for you?
③ ________ sports does she like?
④ ________ does your mother do?
⑤ ________ will you do on the holiday?

6. 밑줄 친 부분을 Whom으로 바꿔 쓸 수 있는 것을 고르세요.

① Who is your close friend?
② What will you get for me?
③ Whose table did you buy?
④ Who invited you to the party?
⑤ Who did you help at the playground?

Words **holiday** 휴일 **close** 가까운; 친한 **playground** 놀이터, 운동장

정답 및 해설 p.14

7. **빈칸에 들어갈 질문으로 가장 알맞은 것을 고르세요.**

A: ______________________

B: I like chicken burgers most.

① Whose food do you like most?
② What will you make for dinner?
③ Who do you give chicken burgers to?
④ Who cooks chicken burgers?
⑤ What food do you like most?

8. **빈칸에 들어갈 말이 바르게 짝지어진 것을 고르세요.**

- A: __________ is the tall man in sportswear?
  B: He is my uncle.
- A: __________ is his job?
  B: He is a basketball player.

① What – Who ② Who – What
③ Who – Whom ④ What – Whom
⑤ Whom – Who

9. **틀린 문장을 고르세요.**

① Whose hairband is that?
② Who sent the e-mails?
③ Whom are you calling?
④ What you did last night?
⑤ Who is the gentleman?

10. **우리말과 영어가 잘못 짝지어진 것을 고르세요.**

① 누가 다리를 건너요?
→ Who crosses the bridge?
② 당신은 오늘 누구를 도와주었나요?
→ Whom did you help today?
③ 그는 무엇을 선택하나요?
→ What does he choose?
④ 그것은 누구의 휴대전화인가요?
→ Whom cell phone is it?
⑤ 그 구름은 무슨 모양인가요?
→ What shape is the cloud?

Words **burger** 버거 **sportswear** 운동복 **job** 일, 직업 **basketball player** 농구선수 **hairband** 머리띠 **gentleman** 신사 **cross** 건너다 **shape** 모양

11. 대화가 어색한 것을 고르세요.

① A: What are you drinking?
B: I'm drinking milk.

② A: Who is your English teacher?
B: It's Mr. Johnson.

③ A: Whose idea was this?
B: It was Jennifer's.

④ A: Whom will he marry?
B: He will marry Tasha.

⑤ A: Who did you see yesterday?
B: I saw a movie.

[12-13] 빈칸에 알맞은 말을 써서 대화를 완성하세요.

서술형

12.

A: __________ __________ __________ __________ for dinner today?
B: I ate Chinese food.

서술형

13.

A: __________ __________ __________ __________ in front of the market?
B: He will meet his younger sister.

서술형

14. 우리말과 같은 뜻이 되도록 주어진 말을 이용하여 문장을 완성하세요.

어제 누가 꽃병을 깼니? (break the vase)

→ ______________________________

서술형

15. 우리말과 같은 뜻이 되도록 주어진 말을 바르게 배열하세요.

너는 학교에서 누구의 책을 빌렸니?
(at school / book / borrow / did / whose / you)

→ ______________________________

Words in front of ~ 앞에 market 시장 vase 꽃병 borrow 빌리다

UNIT 08

where, when, why

Vocab Check! 이번 과에서 배울 단어의 뜻을 확인하고, 모르는 단어에 체크 표시하세요.

√ 1	arrive	동 도착하다	11	in a hurry	서둘러, 급히	21	happen	동 (사건이) 발생하다
2	hospital	명 병원	12	steal	동 훔치다	22	collect	동 모으다
3	roof	명 지붕	13	tie	명 넥타이	23	exercise	동 운동하다
4	accident	명 사고	14	fantastic	형 환상적인	24	last	부 마지막으로
5	hobby	명 취미	15	toothbrush	명 칫솔	25	skip	동 거르다, 빼먹다
6	meeting	명 회의	16	take a walk	산책하다	26	upset	형 화가 난
7	stamp	명 우표	17	stomachache	명 복통	27	dark	형 어두운
8	post office	명 우체국	18	Thailand	명 태국	28	take off	이륙하다
9	get a haircut	이발하다	19	put up	붙이다	29	stadium	명 경기장
10	have a cold	감기에 걸리다	20	poster	명 포스터	30	fever	명 열

UNIT 08 where, when, why

Why did you call the police? – Because I saw a thief.
당신은 왜 경찰에 전화했나요? - 나는 도둑을 봤거든요.

When did you see the thief? – Late at night.
언제 그 도둑을 봤나요? - 늦은 밤에요.

Where did you see the thief? – At home.
어디서 그 도둑을 봤나요? - 집에서요.

A where, when, why

where는 장소, when은 시간, why는 이유를 물을 때 사용하는 의문사예요.

장소 Jack was in the hospital yesterday. (Jack은 어제 병원에 있었어요.)
→ **Where** was Jack yesterday? (Jack은 어제 어디에 있었나요?)

시간 Jack was in the hospital yesterday. (Jack은 어제 병원에 있었어요.)
→ **When** was Jack in the hospital? (Jack은 언제 병원에 있었나요?)

이유 Jack was in the hospital yesterday because he was sick.
(Jack은 아파서 어제 병원에 있었어요.)
→ **Why** was Jack in the hospital yesterday? (왜 Jack은 어제 병원에 있었나요?)

B where

where는 장소나 위치에 관한 정보를 물을 때 사용해요.

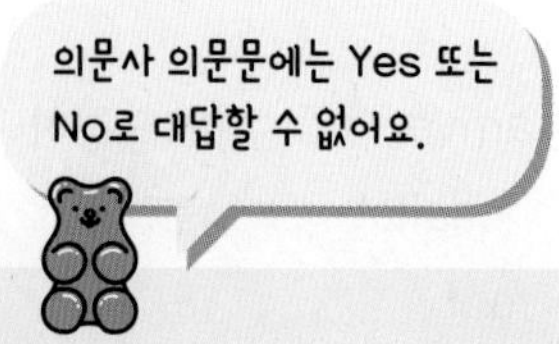

Where (어디에, 어디서)	is	he?	그는 어디에 있나요?
	did	you play tennis?	당신은 어디서 테니스를 쳤나요?

Where were you last night? **Where** do they live?

C when, what time

시간이나 날짜에 관한 정보를 물을 때 when을 사용해요.
구체적인 시각을 물을 때는 what time을 쓰기도 해요.

When (언제)	is	the concert?	그 콘서트는 언제인가요?
What time (몇 시에)	did	you meet him?	당신은 그를 몇 시에 만났나요?

When is her birthday?

What time is the first train?

When[What time] does the musical start?

D why

why는 이유에 관한 정보를 물을 때 사용해요. 주로 because(왜냐하면)를 사용해서 대답해요.

Why (왜)	are	you angry?	당신은 왜 화가 났나요?
	do	they go there?	그들은 왜 그곳에 가나요?

Why are you happy?
– **Because** I got a good grade on the test.

Why do you like that singer?
– **Because** he sings and dances very well.

My Grammar Notes

1 의문사 __________는 장소, __________은 시간, __________는 이유를 물을 때 사용한다.

2 __________ (어디에): __________ do you live?

3 __________ (언제): __________ did you go to bed last night?
→ 구체적인 시간을 물을 때는 when을 __________ __________으로 바꿔 쓸 수 있다.

4 why (왜): Why is he upset?
→ __________로 묻는 의문문에 대한 대답은 보통 __________(왜냐하면)를 이용한다.

Warm-Up

A ( ) 안에서 알맞은 것을 고르세요. where, when, why

1. Where (is / are) my slippers?
2. When (is / are) Children's Day?
3. Why did he (steal / steals) money?
4. When did we (talk / talked) about this?
5. What time did you (get / got) up today?
6. Where (is / does) the baseball stadium?
7. Where (do / does) he usually have lunch?
8. Why (did / was) you start swimming lessons?

Words

slippers 슬리퍼
Children's Day 어린이날
steal 훔치다
stadium 경기장
usually 대개, 보통
coat 코트, 외투
cry 울다
learn 배우다
stay 머무르다
sick 아픈

B 질문에 대한 대답이 적절하면 O, 적절하지 않으면 X 표시하세요. where, when, why

1. Where is your coat? – It's Tony's. X
2. When do you go to school? – Yes, I do.
3. Why is the baby crying? – I don't know.
4. Where were you? – In my room.
5. What time do you go to school? – At 8 a.m.
6. Why did he go home? – He lives in Seoul.
7. Where did you learn English? – No, I didn't.
8. Why do you stay home today? – Because I'm sick.

C 질문에 알맞은 대답을 연결하세요. where, when, why

1. Where did you buy this shirt? •
2. Where is your uncle? •
3. When is your birthday? •
4. Why did you fix your watch? •
5. When does the concert start? •
6. Why was he absent yesterday? •
7. What time does the train leave? •

• ⓐ He's in the U.S.
• ⓑ It leaves at 9:30.
• ⓒ It was broken.
• ⓓ At the mall.
• ⓔ October 1.
• ⓕ He had a cold.
• ⓖ It starts at 7.

Words

fix 고치다, 수리하다
absent 결석한
leave 떠나다
broken 부러진, 고장난
October 10월
have a cold 감기에 걸리다
angry 화가 난
grandparents 조부모님 (할아버지, 할머니)
hairstyle 머리 모양, 헤어스타일
Chinese 중국어

D 우리말과 같은 뜻이 되도록 ( ) 안에서 알맞은 것을 고르세요. where, when, why

1. 네 차는 어디 있니?
   → (When / Where) is your car?
2. 그들은 어디로 갔니?
   → (When / Where) did they go?
3. 너는 왜 화가 났니?
   → (Where / Why) are you so angry?
4. 너는 언제 너의 조부모님을 방문했었니?
   → (When / Why) did you visit your grandparents?
5. 너는 언제 머리 모양을 바꿨니?
   → (Where / When) did you change your hairstyle?
6. 너는 왜 중국어를 공부하고 있니?
   → (Where / Why) are you studying Chinese?

Practice

A ( ) 안에서 알맞은 것을 고르세요.

1. When (was / did) he move to Seoul?
2. Where (is / does) she live?
3. What time (were / did) they meet?
4. Where (is / does) your sister now?
5. Where (do / does) your mom work?
6. Why (are / do) you reading this book?
7. Why (is / does) he study English hard?
8. When (is / does) Thanksgiving Day this year?

B 빈칸에 알맞은 의문사를 보기에서 골라 쓰세요.

보기	when	where	why

1. Where is your cat? – It's on the roof.
2. ______ did you paint it? – Ten minutes ago.
3. ______ do you drink milk? – Every morning.
4. ______ are you running? – I'm late for work.
5. ______ are you eating a lot? – I skipped lunch.
6. ______ did you sleep last night? – On the sofa.
7. ______ did you visit Thailand? – Last year.
8. ______ are you scared? – Because it's too dark.

Words

move 옮기다; 이사하다
Thanksgiving Day 추수감사절
roof 지붕
paint 페인트 칠하다
skip 거르다, 빼먹다
sofa 소파
Thailand 태국
scared 무서워하는
dark 어두운

C 우리말과 같은 뜻이 되도록 빈칸에 알맞은 의문사를 쓰세요.

1. 당신은 왜 웃고 있나요?
   → Why are you laughing?
2. 당신은 어디서 내 강아지를 봤나요?
   → ______ did you see my puppy?
3. Harry의 생일은 언제인가요?
   → ______ is Harry's birthday?
4. 왜 그녀는 늦게 TV를 보고 있나요?
   → ______ is she watching TV late?
5. 당신은 내 열쇠를 어디에 두었나요?
   → ______ did you put my key?

Words

laugh 웃다
puppy 강아지
post office 우체국
street 거리
tie 넥타이
shop 가게
collect 모으다
stamp 우표
hobby 취미
badminton 배드민턴
early in the morning 이른 아침에

D 질문에 알맞은 대답을 고르세요.

1. Where is the post office?
   ① On 7th Street. ② At 6 p.m. ③ In the classroom.
2. Where did he buy his tie?
   ① Two days ago. ② At this shop. ③ He needed it.
3. Why do you collect stamps?
   ① It's my hobby. ② 3 years ago. ③ Yes, I like them.
4. When did you go to the baseball game?
   ① I like baseball. ② Last weekend. ③ At the playground.
5. When do you usually play badminton?
   ① In the park. ② Yesterday. ③ Early in the morning.

E 밑줄 친 부분을 바르게 고쳐 쓰세요.

1. Where is my shoes? → are
2. Why are you love her? →
3. Why does he in a hurry? →
4. What time the bus comes? →
5. Why did you fought with Jack? →
6. When you did take this photo? →
7. Where you spent summer vacation? →
8. When did you sent the text message? →

Words

in a hurry 서둘러, 급히
fight 싸우다 (과거형 **fought**)
take a photo 사진을 찍다
spend (시간을) 보내다 (과거형 **spent**)
summer vacation 여름방학
text message 문자 메시지
class 수업
begin 시작하다
finish 끝나다

F 틀린 부분을 바르게 고쳐 다시 쓰세요.

1. When does the class begins?
   → When does the class begin?
2. Where did you played basketball?
   → ______
3. Why you look so happy?
   → ______
4. What time the show finishes?
   → ______
5. Why you met her yesterday?
   → ______

G 빈칸에 알맞은 말을 써서 밑줄 친 부분을 묻는 의문문을 완성하세요.

1. His toys are in the box.
→ Where are his toys?

2. The baby is in his bed.
→ ______ ______ the baby?

3. I exercise every day because I want to be healthy.
→ ______ ______ you ______ every day?

4. He lost his wallet yesterday.
→ ______ ______ he ______ his wallet?

5. Ally put her book on the desk.
→ ______ ______ Ally ______ her book?

6. The plane took off at 2 p.m.
→ ______ ______ ______ the plane take off?

7. The car accident happened in April.
→ ______ ______ the car accident ______?

8. I had a bad cold, so I went to the hospital.
→ ______ ______ you ______ to the hospital?

9. The meeting starts at 6:30.
→ ______ ______ ______ the meeting ______?

10. New Year's Eve is December 31.
→ ______ ______ New Year's Eve?

11. I called my grandmother last week.
→ ______ ______ you ______ your grandmother?

Words

exercise 운동하다
healthy 건강한
lose 잃어버리다 (과거형 **lost**)
wallet 지갑
plane 비행기
take off 이륙하다
accident 사고
happen (사건이) 발생하다
have a bad cold 심한 감기에 걸리다
hospital 병원
meeting 회의
New Year's Eve 새해 전야 (12월 31일)

Grammar into Writing

A **우리말과 같은 뜻이 되도록 주어진 말을 바르게 배열하세요.**

1. Mark는 지금 어디에 있니? Mark / is / now / where

→ Where is Mark now?

2. 그녀는 왜 웃고 있니? is / she / laughing / why

→ ______________________

3. 너는 아침에 언제 일어나니? do / get up / when / in the morning / you

→ ______________________

4. 그 뮤지컬은 몇 시에 시작하니? what time / the musical / start / does

→ ______________________

5. 너는 어디서 이 사진을 찍었니? this photo / take / did / you / where

→ ______________________

B **우리말과 같은 뜻이 되도록 주어진 말을 이용하여 문장을 완성하세요.**

1. 1) 내 우산은 어디에 있니?

→ Where is my umbrella?

2) 내 양말은 어디에 있니? (socks)

→ Where are my socks?

2. 1) 너는 몇 시에 아침을 먹니?

→ ________ ________ do you eat breakfast?

2) 그는 몇 시에 점심을 먹니? (lunch)

→ ______________________

3. 1) 너는 왜 이 노래를 좋아하니?

→ __________ do you like this song?

2) 그는 왜 이 축구선수를 좋아하니? (soccer player)

→ ____

4. 1) 너는 언제 이 공책을 샀니?

→ __________ did you buy this notebook?

2) Sally는 언제 이 가방을 샀니? (this bag)

→ ____

5. 1) 너는 어디서 그를 만났니?

→ __________ did you meet him?

2) James는 어디서 Sophie를 보았니? (see)

→ ____

C 빈칸에 알맞은 의문사를 넣어 대화를 완성하세요.

A: Hi, Ted. ___Why___ are you putting up posters?

B: Because I lost my puppy.

A: Oh, that's too bad. __________ did you lose it?

B: Yesterday.

A: __________ did you last see it?

B: In the park.

Words **put up** 붙이다 **poster** 포스터, 벽보 **That's too bad.** 참 안됐다. **last** 마지막으로

Wrap-Up Test

1. 영어와 우리말이 잘못 짝지어진 것을 고르세요.

① when - 언제　② where - 어떻게
③ why - 왜　⑤ what time - 몇 시에
④ whose - 누구의

[2-4] 빈칸에 알맞은 말을 고르세요.

2.

A: _______ do you usually take a walk?
B: After lunch.

① Who　② When
③ Where　④ Why
⑤ What

3.

A: _______ are they swimming?
B: In the pool.

① What　② When
③ Where　④ Why
⑤ What time

4.

A: _______ do you have a stomachache?
B: I ate some bad eggs last night.

① Who　② When
③ Where　④ Why
⑤ What time

5. 빈칸에 알맞은 말이 바르게 짝지어진 것을 고르세요.

A: _______ does your aunt live?
B: She lives in Jeju.
A: _______ did you visit your cousins?
B: I visited them last winter.

① When – Why　② Where – Why
③ Why – When　④ When – Where
⑤ Where – When

Words　**take a walk** 산책하다　**pool** 수영장　**stomachache** 복통　**cousin** 사촌

6. 질문에 대한 대답으로 알맞지 않은 것을 고르세요.

When did you read the book *Matilda*?

① Last month.

② I didn't read it.

③ About two weeks ago.

④ That's a fantastic book.

⑤ Yesterday.

7. 틀린 문장을 고르세요.

① When is Halloween?

② Where do you usually study?

③ Why did you buy this cake?

④ What time you go to the school?

⑤ When can they play the game?

8. 우리말을 영어로 바르게 옮긴 것을 고르세요.

그 상점은 언제 문을 닫나요?

① When the store closed?

② When do the store closes?

③ When does the store close?

④ When does the store closed?

⑤ When does the store closes?

9. 밑줄 친 부분을 바르게 고친 것을 고르세요.

A: When did they visit the theater?
B: Because they wanted to see the movie.
A: Why will you be at the library?
B: I think it will be around 4 p.m.

① Why – What
② Where – Where
③ Why – Where
④ Why – What time
⑤ What time – When

10. 대화가 어색한 것을 고르세요.

① A: Why did you catch a cold?
B: I have a fever.

② A: Why are you angry?
B: My brother broke my robot.

③ A: Where is my toothbrush?
B: It's on the table.

④ A: When did you get a haircut?
B: Last weekend.

⑤ A: What time will you come back?
B: I think around 7 o'clock.

Words **fantastic** 환상적인 **Halloween** 핼러윈 **catch a cold** 감기에 걸리다 **fever** 열 **toothbrush** 칫솔 **get a haircut** 이발하다

서술형

11. 빈칸에 들어갈 수 없는 것을 고르세요.

A: ______________________

B: I was sitting on a bench at a park last night.

① Where were you sitting last night?

② Why were you sitting on the bench?

③ What were you doing at a park?

④ Who was sitting on the bench last night?

⑤ When were you sitting on the bench?

서술형

12. 빈칸에 알맞은 말을 써서 대화를 완성하세요.

A: ________ ________ ________ ________ his wallet?

B: He found it on the school bus.

서술형

13. 우리말과 같은 뜻이 되도록 주어진 말을 이용하여 문장을 완성하세요.

그 기차는 몇 시에 출발하니?

(leave, what, the train)

→ ______________________

____

서술형

14. 주어진 단어를 이용하여 대답에 알맞은 질문을 완성하세요.

A: ________ ________ ________ at the gym? (be)

B: Because she wanted to get healthy.

서술형

15. 우리말과 같은 뜻이 되도록 주어진 말을 바르게 배열하세요.

너는 언제 공항에 도착했니?

(arrive / did / when / you / at the airport)

→ ______________________

____

Words **gym** 체육관 **arrive** 도착하다 **airport** 공항

UNIT 09

how

Vocab Check! 이번 과에서 배울 단어의 뜻을 확인하고, 모르는 단어에 체크 표시하세요.

1	exam	명 시험	11	guest	명 손님	21	exhibition	명 전시회
2	leave	동 떠나다	12	tower	명 탑, 타워	22	building	명 건물
3	free time	자유 시간	13	summer	명 여름	23	peach	명 복숭아
4	word	명 단어	14	grow	동 자라다	24	cereal	명 시리얼
5	run	동 달리다; 운행하다	15	penguin	명 펭귄	25	spider	명 거미
6	monitor	명 모니터, 화면	16	poem	명 시	26	turtle	명 거북
7	wait for	~를 기다리다	17	save	동 모으다; 구하다	27	mango	명 망고
8	last	동 계속되다	18	daughter	명 딸	28	once	부 한 번
9	taekwondo	명 태권도	19	need	동 필요하다	29	life	명 생명, 목숨
10	take a shower	샤워하다	20	carry	동 나르다	30	lesson	명 강습

UNIT 09 how

How **was your trip to Hawaii?** – It was **nice**.
하와이 여행은 어땠나요? - 좋았어요.

How long **did you stay there?** – **A week**.
당신은 그곳에 얼마나 오래 머물렀나요? - 일주일이요.

How much **money did you spend?** – **$5,000**.
당신은 얼마나 많은 돈을 썼나요? - 5천 달러요.

A how

how는 상태나 방법, 수단 등의 정보를 물어볼 때 사용해요.

How 어떻게, 얼마나	is	the weather? (상태)	날씨가 어떤가요?
	did	you get to school? (방법, 수단)	당신은 어떻게 학교에 갔나요?

B how + 형용사/부사: 얼마나 ~한(~하게)

의문사 how 뒤에 형용사나 부사를 써서 나이, 횟수, 기간 등의 정보를 물을 수 있어요.

How old (얼마나 나이 든[오래된])	are	you? (나이)	당신은 몇 살인가요?
How tall (얼마나 (키가) 큰)	is	he? (키)	그는 키가 얼마나 큰가요?
How often (얼마나 자주)	do	you go hiking? (횟수)	당신은 얼마나 자주 하이킹을 가나요?
How long (얼마나 긴)	is	the river? (길이)	그 강은 얼마나 긴가요?
How long (얼마나 오래)	did	you live there? (기간)	당신은 그곳에서 얼마나 오래 살았나요?

C how many, how much

의문사 how 뒤에 many와 much를 써서 수량과 가격을 물을 수 있어요.

1. how many / how much + 명사

수를 물을 때는 'how many + 복수명사'를, 양을 물을 때는 'how much + 셀 수 없는 명사'를 사용해요.

How many (얼마나 많은)	books (복수명사)	are in the bookshop?	서점에 얼마나 많은 책이 있나요?
		did you read?	당신은 얼마나 많은 책을 읽었나요?
How much (얼마나 많은)	water (셀 수 없는 명사)	is in the cup?	컵 속에 얼마나 많은 물이 있나요?
		do you drink?	당신은 얼마나 많은 물을 마시나요?

How many **students** are in the classroom?
복수명사

How much **salt** did you put in the soup?
셀 수 없는 명사

2. how much

how much는 가격을 물을 때도 쓸 수 있어요.

How much (얼마)	are	those roses?	저 장미들은 (가격이) 얼마인가요?

How much is this pencil case? How much are these blue jeans?

My Grammar Notes

1 __________는 '어떻게'의 뜻으로 방법이나 상태를 묻는 의문사이다.

2 how + 형용사[부사]: 얼마나 ~한[하게]
(1) how old (얼마나 나이 든 / 얼마나 오래된) (2) ______________ (얼마나 키가 큰)
(3) ______________ (얼마나 자주) (4) ______________ (얼마나 긴 / 얼마나 오래)

3 how many는 수를 물을 때, how much는 양을 물을 때 쓴다.
______________ + 복수명사 ______________ + 셀 수 없는 명사

4 how __________는 가격을 물을 때 사용한다.

Warm-Up

A How를 쓸 수 있는 문장에 V 표시하세요. how

1.	How	tall is she?	V
2.		long is the song?	
3.		sports do you like?	
4.		old is your grandmother?	
5.		time are we going to leave?	
6.		often does he take a shower?	
7.		do you get to school every day?	
8.		played the piano last night?	

Words

leave 떠나다
take a shower 샤워하다
invite 초대하다

B ( ) 안에서 알맞은 것을 고르세요. how many, how much

1. How (many / much) juice did you drink?
2. How (many / much) cats do you have?
3. How (many / much) cheese did you eat?
4. How (many / much) toy robots does he have?
5. How (many / much) money do you want?
6. How (many / much) friends did you invite?
7. How (many / much) bread do you eat every day?
8. How (many / much) students are there in your school?

C 빈칸에 알맞은 말을 보기에서 골라 쓰세요. how + 형용사/부사

보기 old tall often long many much

1. How old is your little brother? – He is 3 years old.
2. How ______ is the tree? – It's about 8 meters.
3. How ______ is your vacation? – A month.
4. How ______ do you go swimming? – Twice a week.
5. How ______ is this backpack? – It's 50,000 won.
6. How ______ people are in the car? – Four.
7. How ______ time do you need? – Just 10 minutes.

Words

about 대략
vacation 방학
twice 두 번
backpack 배낭
last 계속되다
exciting 흥미진진한
get a haircut 머리를 깎다
once 한 번

D 질문에 알맞은 대답을 연결하세요. how

1. How old is Jessica? • • ⓐ I'm 165 cm.
2. How tall are you? • • ⓑ She is 20.
3. How many dogs do you have? • • ⓒ Two hours.
4. How much is the ticket? • • ⓓ It's $30.
5. How long did the concert last? • • ⓔ I have two dogs.
6. How was your holiday? • • ⓕ It was exciting.
7. How often do you get a haircut? • • ⓖ I studied hard.
8. How did you pass the exam? • • ⓗ Once a month.

Practice

A 질문에 알맞은 대답을 보기에서 고르세요.

보기 ⓐ I had a key. ⓑ About a month. ⓒ There are five.
ⓓ 500 dollars. ⓔ It's 300 meters. ⓕ Once a week.

1. How tall is this tower? ⓔ
2. How often do you eat out?
3. How did you open the door?
4. How long did you stay in Berlin?
5. How much is this washing machine?
6. How many birds are there in the cage?

Words

tower 탑, 타워
eat out 외식하다
Berlin (독일) 베를린
washing machine 세탁기
cage 새장
turtle 거북
daughter 딸
guest 손님
remember 기억하다

B ( ) 안에서 알맞은 것을 고르세요.

1. How old (are / is) these turtles?
2. How (is / does) she feel about me?
3. How long (are / do) you sleep a day?
4. How often (are / do) they go shopping?
5. How old (is / does) your daughter?
6. How tall (are / is) that basketball player?
7. How many guests (are / do) at the party?
8. How (were / did) you remember his birthday?

C 빈칸에 들어갈 수 없는 말을 고르세요.

1. How many ____ do you have? ☐ belts ☐ hats ☑ time
2. How much ____ do you want? ☐ tea ☐ butter ☐ chairs
3. How many ____ can you carry? ☐ boxes ☐ money ☐ books
4. How many ____ are in Korea? ☐ dog ☐ people ☐ parks
5. How much ____ does he need? ☐ pens ☐ water ☐ salt
6. How much ____ did you eat? ☐ rice ☐ eggs ☐ cereal

Words

carry 가지고 다니다, 나르다
salt 소금
cereal 시리얼
penguin 펭귄
zoo 동물원
go fishing 낚시하러 가다
wait for ~를 기다리다

D 우리말과 같은 뜻이 되도록 빈칸에 알맞은 말을 쓰세요.

1. 동물원에는 얼마나 많은 펭귄들이 있나요?
→ How many penguins are there in the zoo?
2. 당신의 고양이는 몇 살인가요?
→ ____ ____ is your cat?
3. 너희 아버지는 얼마나 자주 낚시하러 가시니?
→ ____ ____ does your father go fishing?
4. 이 컴퓨터는 얼마인가요?
→ ____ ____ is this computer?
5. 너는 얼마나 오래 나를 기다렸니?
→ ____ ____ did you wait for me?
6. 너는 커피에 얼마나 많은 설탕을 넣었니?
→ ____ ____ sugar did you put in your coffee?

E how를 이용하여 빈칸에 알맞은 말을 쓰세요.

1. A: How old is that building?
   B: It's 100 years old.
2. A: ______ is the tennis player?
   B: She is 175 cm.
3. A: ______ was your summer vacation?
   B: It was great!
4. A: ______ are these rain boots?
   B: They are only 20 dollars.
5. A: ______ is this bridge?
   B: It's 800 meters.
6. A: ______ English words do you know?
   B: About 500 words.
7. A: ______ did he win the gold medal?
   B: He practiced a lot.
8. A: ______ coffee do you drink a day?
   B: Two cups of coffee.
9. A: ______ times a day do you brush your teeth?
   B: Three times.
10. A: ______ does she have taekwondo lessons?
    B: Twice a week.
11. A: ______ do you spend your free time?
    B: I usually sleep.

Words

building 건물
summer 여름
rain boots 장화
bridge 다리
word 단어
win a gold medal 금메달을 따다
practice 연습하다
brush one's teeth 이를 닦다
taekwondo 태권도
lesson 강습
free time 자유 시간

F 빈칸에 알맞은 말을 써서 밑줄 친 부분을 묻는 의문문을 완성하세요.

1. It's cloudy today.
→ How is the weather today?

2. He goes hiking once a week.
→ ______ ______ ______ he go hiking?

3. He needs a lot of money.
→ ______ ______ money ______ he need?

4. David is 145 cm tall.
→ ______ ______ ______ David?

5. I stayed in Japan for ten days.
→ ______ ______ ______ you stay in Japan?

6. She went there on foot.
→ ______ ______ she get there?

7. Peter has six sneakers.
→ ______ ______ sneakers ______ Peter have?

8. My cousin is 13 years old.
→ ______ ______ ______ your cousin?

9. This hat is 10 dollars.
→ ______ ______ ______ this hat?

10. I traveled to seven countries.
→ ______ ______ countries ______ you travel to?

11. It was pretty good.
→ ______ ______ the exhibition?

Words

cloudy 흐린
weather 날씨
hiking 도보 여행
need 필요하다
stay 머무르다
on foot 걸어서
travel 여행하다
country 나라
pretty 예쁜; 어느 정도, 꽤
exhibition 전시회

Grammar into Writing

A 우리말과 같은 뜻이 되도록 주어진 말을 바르게 배열하세요.

1. 이 반지는 얼마인가요? this ring / is / how / much

→ How much is this ring?

2. 서울 타워는 얼마나 높니? tall / Seoul Tower / how / is

→ ______________________

3. 너는 얼마나 많은 쿠키를 먹었니? how / did / you / cookies / many / eat

→ ______________________

4. 너는 얼마나 자주 축구를 하니? how / do / often / soccer / play / you

→ ______________________

5. 당신은 어떻게 이 케이크를 만들었나요? how / you / make / did / this cake

→ ______________________

B 우리말과 같은 뜻이 되도록 주어진 말을 이용하여 문장을 완성하세요.

1. 1) 너는 얼마나 많은 돈을 모았니?

→ How much money did you save?

2) 너는 얼마나 많은 우유를 마셨니? (milk, drink)

→ How much milk did you drink?

2. 1) 이 버스는 얼마나 자주 운행하나요?

→ ________ ________ does this bus run?

2) 이 지하철은 얼마나 자주 운행하나요? (this subway)

→ ______________________

3. 1) 이 키보드는 얼마인가요?

→ ________ ________ is this keyboard?

2) 이 모니터는 얼마인가요? (this monitor)

→ ________________________________

4. 1) 그 강은 얼마나 긴가요?

→ ________ ________ is the river?

2) 만리장성은 얼마나 긴가요? (the Great Wall)

→ ________________________________

5. 1) 그 호텔에는 얼마나 많은 방이 있나요?

→ ________ ________ rooms are there in the hotel?

2) 은하수에는 얼마나 많은 별들이 있나요? (stars, the Milky Way)

→ ________________________________

C 빈칸에 알맞은 말을 써서 대화를 완성하세요.

A: Congratulations! ____How do you____ feel?

B: I can't believe it. I feel happy!

A: ________________ practice?

B: I practiced every day. I ran a lot.

A: ________________ run a day?

B: I ran 3 hours a day.

Words
ring 반지 **save** 모으다; 구하다 **run** 달리다; 운행하다 **keyboard** 키보드
monitor 모니터, 화면 **the Great Wall** (중국) 만리장성 **the Milky Way** 은하수
Congratulations! 축하합니다!

Wrap-Up Test

1. 영어와 우리말이 잘못 짝지어진 것을 고르세요.

① how - 어떻게

② how long - 얼마나 오래

③ how often - 얼마나 자주

④ how many - 얼마나 비싼

⑤ how old - 얼마나 나이 든

[2-3] 빈칸에 들어갈 수 없는 것을 고르세요.

2.

How much ________ did you buy?

① rice ② sugar

③ butter ④ peaches

⑤ cheese

3.

How many ________ does she have?

① jackets ② bags

③ money ④ shirts

⑤ hats

[4-5] 빈칸에 알맞은 말을 고르세요.

4.

A: ______________ was your exam?
B: It was very difficult.

① How ② How old

③ How tall ④ How much

⑤ How long

5.

A: ______________ do you call Jihee?
B: Every day.

① How old ② How tall

③ How long ④ How often

⑤ How many

6. 질문에 대한 대답으로 알맞지 않은 것을 고르세요.

How long did you play baseball these days?

① For two hours. ② I don't know.

③ Every day. ④ Only 20 minutes.

⑤ About half an hour.

Words **peach** 복숭아 **exam** 시험 **difficult** 어려운 **call** 전화하다 **half an hour** 30분

7. 빈칸에 How가 들어갈 수 없는 것을 고르세요.

① _________ long did you sleep?

② _________ did you hear the news?

③ _________ wallet is this?

④ _________ many oranges are there?

⑤ _________ much juice do you need?

8. 빈칸에 알맞은 말이 바르게 짝지어진 것을 고르세요.

A: _______________ are you feeling now?

B: I'm still feeling sick.

A: _______________ days do you have to stay in the hospital?

① How – How much

② How – How many

③ What – How many

④ What – How often

⑤ How – How

9. 틀린 문장을 고르세요.

① How long is the river?

② How does the plant grow?

③ How much bread do they eat?

④ How much are these mangoes?

⑤ How many are bikes in the park?

10. 우리말을 영어로 바르게 옮긴 것을 고르세요.

그 산은 얼마나 높습니까?

① How is the mountain?

② How old is the mountain?

③ How tall is the mountain?

④ How often is the mountain?

⑤ How much is the mountain?

Words **hear** 듣다 **sick** 아픈 **plant** 심다; 식물 **grow** 자라다 **mango** 망고 (복수형 **mangoes**) **mountain** 산

11. 대화가 어색한 것을 고르세요.

① A: How long did you study math?
B: I studied for three hours.

② A: How many legs does a spider have?
B: It has eight legs.

③ A: How was the movie?
B: It was boring.

④ A: How much is this car?
B: I only have one car.

⑤ A: How do you feel about the poem?
B: It is really great!

[12-13] 빈칸에 알맞은 말을 써서 대화를 완성하세요.

서술형

12.

A: __________ __________ do you eat out?
B: Three times a week.

서술형

13.

A: __________ __________ is the washing machine?
B: It's 700 dollars.

서술형

14. 우리말과 같은 뜻이 되도록 주어진 말을 이용하여 문장을 완성하세요.

당신은 어떻게 그의 목숨을 구했나요? (save)

→ ________________________________ his life?

서술형

15. 우리말과 같은 뜻이 되도록 빈칸에 알맞은 말을 쓰세요.

__________ __________ __________ __________ in the kitchen?
(부엌에는 얼마나 많은 바나나가 있나요?)

Words math 수학 spider 거미 boring 지루한 poem 시 life 생명, 목숨 kitchen 부엌

UNIT 10

비인칭 주어 it

Vocab Check! 이번 과에서 배울 단어의 뜻을 확인하고, 모르는 단어에 체크 표시하세요.

1	favorite	형 가장 좋아하는	11	autumn	명 가을	21	left	명 왼쪽
2	doll	명 인형	12	outside	부 밖에	22	bakery	명 빵집
3	already	부 이미, 벌써	13	Vietnam	명 베트남	23	hard	부 열심히; 심하게
4	snowy	형 눈이 오는	14	Australia	명 호주	24	far	부 멀리
5	calendar	명 달력	15	fan	명 선풍기	25	ticket	명 표
6	late	부 늦게	16	noon	명 정오, 낮 12시	26	passport	명 여권
7	soon	부 곧	17	sell	동 팔다	27	warm	형 따뜻한
8	dry	형 건조한	18	village	명 마을	28	foggy	형 안개가 낀
9	freezing	형 몹시 추운	19	almost	부 거의	29	theater	명 극장
10	put on	~을 입다	20	wonderful	형 멋진	30	way	명 방법; 길

UNIT 10 비인칭 주어 it

It's May 5.
5월 5일이에요.

It's Children's Day.
어린이날이에요.

It's sunny today.
오늘은 날씨가 화창해요.

A 비인칭 주어 it *vs.* 대명사 it

it은 '그것'이라는 뜻의 대명사로 쓰이기도 하지만, 시간이나 날짜, 거리 등을 나타내는 비인칭 주어로도 쓰여요. 이때 it은 별다른 뜻이 없으므로 해석하지 않아요.

대명사 it	그것	What is it? (그것은 무엇인가요?) – It's a new clock. (그것은 새 시계예요.)
비인칭 주어 it	–	What time is it? (몇 시인가요?) – It's 8 a.m. (오전 8시예요.)

B 시간, 날짜, 요일의 it 참고 3권 부록

비인칭 주어 it은 시간, 날짜, 요일 등에 대해 묻고 답할 때 쓸 수 있어요.

시간	What time is it now? (지금 몇 시인가요?)	It's 7 p.m. It's 5:30. It's 10 o'clock.
날짜	What is the date today? (오늘은 며칠인가요?)	It's April 1(st). It's July 10(th). It's August 28(th).
요일	What day is it today? (오늘은 무슨 요일인가요?)	It's Monday. It's Sunday. It's Saturday.

이외에도 날씨는 나타내는 단어에는 windy (바람이 부는), hot (더운), cool (시원한) 등이 있어요.

C 날씨, 계절의 it 참고 Unit 05

비인칭 주어 it은 날씨나 계절에 대해 묻고 답할 때도 사용할 수 있어요.

날씨	How is the weather? = What's the weather like? (날씨가 어떤가요?)	It's sunny. It's cold. It's rainy.	It's cloudy. It's warm. It's snowy.
계절	What season is it? (무슨 계절인가요?)	It's spring. It's fall[autumn].	It's summer. It's winter.

D 거리의 it

비인칭 주어 it은 거리를 나타낼 때도 쓸 수 있어요.

거리	How far is it? (거리가 얼마나 먼가요?)	It's 8 miles. It's 10 kilometers. It's 5 km from here to the library.

Mini Grammar 참고 3권 Unit 09

날짜를 읽을 때 일(日)의 마지막 숫자가 one, two, three로 읽힐 경우 1일은 1st (first), 2일은 2nd (second), 3일은 3rd (third)로 표기하고, 4일 이후부터는 숫자 뒤에 th를 붙여서 나타내요. 월(月)과 함께 숫자로 표기할 때는 숫자 뒤의 두 글자(st, nd, rd, th)를 생략하기도 해요.

1일: 1st / first	2일: 2nd / second	3일: 3rd / third
4일: 4th / fourth	5일: 5th / fifth	10일: 10th / tenth
1월 1일: January 1(st)	2월 2일: February 2(nd)	3월 3일: March 3(rd)
4월 4일: April 4(th)	5월 11일: May 11(th)	6월 12일: June 12(th)

My Grammar Notes

1 시간, 날짜, 날씨, 거리 등은 비인칭 주어 ________을 써서 나타낸다.

2 시간: ________ is 5 o'clock now. (지금은 5시다.)

3 요일: What ________ is ________ today? (오늘은 무슨 요일인가요?)

4 날씨: ________ will be ________ tomorrow. (내일 비가 올 것이다.)

5 거리: How far ________ ________? (얼마나 먼가요?)

Warm-Up

A itО 비인칭 주어이면 O, 대명사이면 X 표시하세요.

비인칭 주어, 대명사

1. It's spring. O
2. It is my blog.
3. It isn't my diary.
4. It's ten thirty now.
5. It is my favorite doll.
6. It rained yesterday.
7. What day is it today?
8. It was Sunday yesterday.

Words

spring 봄
blog 블로그
diary 일기장
favorite 가장 좋아하는
doll 인형
snowy 눈이 오는
London (영국) 런던
kilometer (= km) 킬로미터

B 밑줄 친 it의 쓰임을 보기에서 골라 쓰세요.

비인칭 주어 it

보기 ⓐ 날씨 ⓑ 계절 ⓒ 시간 ⓓ 날짜 ⓔ 요일 ⓕ 거리

1. It's winter. ⓑ
2. Is it Tuesday?
3. It's August 3rd.
4. What time is it?
5. It was Wednesday.
6. It is seven fifty now.
7. Is it snowy in London?
8. It's 7 kilometers from here.

C 우리말을 영어로 바르게 옮긴 것은 O, 틀린 것은 X 표시하세요.

비인칭 주어 it

1. 오늘은 따뜻하다. → This is warm today. X
2. 지금은 가을이다. → It is autumn now.
3. 여기에 매우 가깝다. → It's very close to here.
4. 오늘은 목요일이다. → It's Thursday today.
5. 지금 몇 시니? → What time is that now?
6. 눈이 올 것이다. → It's going to snow.
7. 오늘은 11월 14일이다. → It's November 14.
8. 지금은 4시 30분이다. → Now is four thirty.
9. 어제는 비가 왔다. → Yesterday rained.
10. 그가 돌아왔을 때는 5시였다.
    → It was 5 o'clock when he came back.

Words

warm 따뜻한
autumn 가을
close 가까운
snow 눈; 눈이 오다
far 멀리
weather 날씨
season 계절

D 질문에 대한 알맞은 대답을 연결하세요.

비인칭 주어 it

1. What day is it today? • - - - - • ⓐ It's Sunday.
2. What time is it now? • • ⓑ It's 3 km.
3. How far is it from here? • • ⓒ It's March 2nd.
4. What is the date today? • • ⓓ It's summer.
5. How is the weather? • • ⓔ It's 10 o'clock.
6. What season is it? • • ⓕ It's sunny.

Practice

A 우리말과 같은 뜻이 되도록 ( ) 안에서 알맞은 것을 고르세요.

1. 6시 30분이다. → (It / This) is six thirty.
2. 월요일이다. → (It / This) is Monday.
3. 이것은 달력이다. → (This / It) is a calendar.
4. 오늘은 7월 22일이다. → (It / Now) is July 22nd today.
5. 한국은 봄이다. → (Here / It) is spring in Korea.
6. 싱가포르에는 단 한 계절만 있다.
   → (It / There) is only one season in Singapore.

Words

calendar 달력
Singapore 싱가포르
outside 밖에
rain 비; 비가 오다
a lot 많이
interesting 흥미로운
ticket 표
freezing 몹시 추운
Australia 호주
passport 여권

B 밑줄 친 it의 쓰임이 나머지와 다른 것을 고르세요.

1. ① It's windy outside.
   ② It's my ball.
   ③ It's 12 o'clock.
   ④ What day is it today?

2. ① What time is it?
   ② Do you like it?
   ③ How was it?
   ④ Where did you see it?

3. ① It's winter.
   ② It's raining a lot.
   ③ It's a beautiful flower.
   ④ What season is it now?

4. ① It was interesting.
   ② It's so small.
   ③ It's my ticket.
   ④ It's 5 km from here.

5. ① It's my car.
   ② It's ten twenty now.
   ③ It was freezing yesterday.
   ④ It is autumn in Australia.

6. ① It's Saturday.
   ② Is it your passport?
   ③ It's February 18.
   ④ How far is it?

C 질문에 대한 대답으로 알맞은 것을 고르세요.

1. What day is it today?
   ① It's Friday. ② It's two forty.
   ③ It's for three days. ④ It's 3 km.

2. What time is it?
   ① It's 4 p.m. ② It takes 10 minutes.
   ③ I don't have time. ④ It's my watch.

3. What is the date today?
   ① It's Saturday. ② It's a beautiful day.
   ③ In October. ④ It's November 11th.

4. What's the weather like?
   ① It's fall. ② It's 4 p.m.
   ③ It's snowy. ④ I caught a cold.

5. How far is the subway station from here?
   ① By bike. ② It's about 100 meters.
   ③ For two days. ④ It's on your left.

Words

take (시간이) 걸리다
minute (시간) 분
catch a cold 감기에 걸리다
subway station 지하철 역
about 대략
meter 미터
left 왼쪽
soon 곧

D 빈칸에 알맞은 말을 쓰세요.

1. A: What time ____ is ____ it ____ now?
   B: ____ It ____ is ____ ten o'clock.

2. A: What ________ is ________ tomorrow?
   B: It's Wednesday.

3. A: How's the weather in Tokyo?
   B: Very cloudy. ________ ________ going to rain soon.

4. A: How ________ is ________ from here to your house?
   B: ________ ________ 1 kilometer.

E 우리말과 같은 뜻이 되도록 빈칸에 알맞은 말을 쓰세요.

Words

already 이미, 벌써
last 지난
theater 극장

1. 곧 눈이 올 것이다.
   → It is going to snow soon.
2. 오늘은 무슨 요일입니까?
   → ______ ______ is ______ today?
3. 어제는 매우 따뜻했다.
   → ______ ______ so ______ yesterday.
4. 오늘은 11월 23일이다.
   → ______ ______ November 23rd today.
5. 지금 몇 시예요?
   → ______ ______ is ______ now?
6. 내일은 일요일이다.
   → ______ ______ Sunday tomorrow.
7. 벌써 8시 10분이다.
   → ______ ______ already ______ ten.
8. 버스로 두 시간 걸려요.
   → ______ takes 2 hours by bus.
9. 우리 집에서 멀다.
   → ______ ______ ______ from my house.
10. 지난 여름에는 비가 많이 왔다.
    → ______ ______ a lot last summer.
11. 극장까지 2 km이다.
    → ______ ______ 2 km to the theater.
12. 서울에서 부산까지 얼마나 먼가요?
    → How far ______ ______ from Seoul to Busan?

F 주어진 말을 바르게 배열하세요.

Words

Vietnam 베트남
village 마을

1. (wasn't / it / very windy / yesterday)
→ It wasn't very windy yesterday.

2. (cold / is / it / getting)
→ ______.

3. (far / is / how / it / from here)
→ ______?

4. (Thursday / it / not / is)
→ ______.

5. (the date / today / is / what)
→ ______?

6. (it / season / what / is / in Vietnam)
→ ______?

7. (hot / is / in summer / it)
→ ______.

8. (now / 11:20 / is / it)
→ ______.

9. (it / now / what / is / time)
→ ______?

10. (far / from here / to the village / it's)
→ ______.

11. (is / it / to / close / here)
→ ______.

12. (of January / the second / Sunday / it's)
→ ______.

Grammar into Writing

A 어울리는 문장끼리 선으로 연결한 뒤, 우리말로 해석하세요.

1. It's December 24th today. •	• ⓐ Bring an umbrella.
2. It's very cold outside. •	• ⓑ Merry Christmas!
3. It's Friday night. •	• ⓒ Let's go to the movies.
4. It's going to rain at night. •	• ⓓ I will buy a fan.
5. It's far from here to the market. •	• ⓔ Take a bus.
6. It's already summer. •	• ⓕ Let's have lunch.
7. It's 12 o'clock now. •	• ⓖ Put on your coat.

1. 오늘은 12월 24일이야. 메리 크리스마스!
2.
3.
4.
5.
6.
7.

B 우리말과 같은 뜻이 되도록 빈칸에 알맞은 말을 쓰세요.

1. 오늘은 날씨가 덥다.

→ It is hot today.

2. 내일은 무슨 요일인가요?

→ ________ ________ ________ ________ tomorrow?

3. 여기서부터 그 도시까지는 멀다.

→ ________ ________ ________from here to the city.

4. 어제는 내 생일이었다.

→ ________ ________ my birthday yesterday.

5. 캐나다는 지금 여름이다.

→ ________ ________ ________ in Canada now.

6. 밖이 추운가요?

→ ________ ________ cold outside?

C 다음 글을 읽고, 밑줄 친 부분을 바르게 고쳐 쓰세요.

Sam and I rode bikes in the mountains yesterday. ❶ This was warm and sunny. At first, we were very excited. But ❷ that was far from our house. We arrived home very late. ❸ There was almost 8 p.m. We were very tired.

↓

❶ It was ________________________________

❷ ________________________________

❸ ________________________________

Words **market** 시장 **fan** 선풍기 **put on** ~을 입다 **ride** 타다 (과거형 **rode**) **excited** 신이 난 **arrive** 도착하다 **late** 늦게 **almost** 거의 **tired** 피곤한

Wrap-Up Test

[1-2] 밑줄 친 it의 쓰임이 나머지와 다른 것을 고르세요.

1.

① It's Saturday.

② It's a wonderful day.

③ It's a present for you.

④ It's 3:45 now.

⑤ It's 4 miles to the lake.

2.

① It was noon.

② How far is it?

③ What season is it?

④ It will be December 25.

⑤ Who will bring it tomorrow?

3. 빈칸에 알맞은 말이 바르게 짝지어진 것을 고르세요.

A: What is the __________ today?

B: __________ is April 1.

① day – It
② date – It
③ time – That
④ weather – That
⑤ month – This

[4-6] 질문에 대한 대답으로 알맞은 것을 고르세요.

4.

What's the weather like?

① It's winter.

② It's August 30.

③ It's raining hard.

④ It's not far from here.

⑤ I don't like the weather.

Words **wonderful** 멋진 **present** 선물 **mile** (거리) 마일 **lake** 호수 **noon** 정오, 낮 12시 **hard** 열심히; 심하게

5.

How far is it to the bookstore?

① It sells a lot of books.
② It is a very tall building.
③ Books are good for you.
④ It is a long way from your house.
⑤ You can read books at the library.

6.

What time is it now?

① It needs some time.
② It is 7:05.
③ It's 60 dollars.
④ It takes about 5 minutes.
⑤ It will not take much time.

서술형

7. 빈칸에 알맞은 말을 써서 대화를 완성하세요.

A: __________ __________ __________ __________ from here to the airport?
B: It's about 4 kilometers.

8. 빈칸에 It[it]이 들어갈 수 없는 것을 고르세요.

① __________ like spring.
② __________ is Monday today.
③ __________ is windy and cold.
④ Is __________ foggy in Japan?
⑤ __________ is 60 kilometers from here.

9. 두 문장이 같은 뜻이 되도록 빈칸에 알맞은 것을 고르세요.

What's the weather like today?
= __________ is the weather today?

① What ② How
③ Why ④ Who
⑤ When

10. 밑줄 친 부분 중 비인칭 주어 it이 아닌 것을 고르세요.

① It was January 1st yesterday. ② It snowed a lot. ③ It was freezing. ④ It was 8 o'clock in the morning, but I went outside and made a snowman. ⑤ It was big and fat!

Words sell 팔다 way 방법; 길 foggy 안개가 낀 snowman 눈사람 airport 공항

11. 우리말과 영어가 잘못 짝지어진 것을 고르세요.

① 곧 눈이 올 것이다.
→ It's going to snow soon.

② 오늘은 10월 4일이다.
→ It's October 4 today.

③ 지금은 6시 20분이다.
→ It's 6:20 now.

④ 병원까지는 별로 멀지 않다.
→ This is not so far to the hospital.

⑤ 오늘은 무슨 요일입니까?
→ What day is it today?

12. 대화가 어색한 것을 고르세요.

① A: What season is it?
B: It's hot and dry.

② A: What day is it?
B: It's Wednesday.

③ A: What time is it?
B: It's seven o'clock.

④ A: Let's go on a picnic.
B: That's not a good idea. It's rainy.

⑤ A: Where is the bakery?
B: It's in the shopping mall.

서술형

13. 틀린 부분을 찾아 바르게 고쳐 쓰세요.

A: What time is it now?
B: This is ten ten.

→ ______________________

서술형

14. 우리말과 같은 뜻이 되도록 주어진 말을 바르게 배열하세요.

오늘은 맑고 따뜻하겠습니다.
(sunny and warm / be / it / will / today)

→ ______________________
____

서술형

15. 우리말과 같은 뜻이 되도록 주어진 말을 이용하여 대화를 완성하세요.

A: ______________________
______________________ (season)
(무슨 계절입니까?)
B: It's summer.
(여름입니다.)

Words dry 건조한 go on a picnic 소풍 가다 bakery 빵집

부록

1 동사의 3인칭 단수 변화형과 동사원형-ing형

동사원형		3인칭 단수 변화형	-ing형
bake	굽다	bakes	baking
become	~이 되다	becomes	becoming
begin	시작하다	begins	beginning
borrow	빌리다	borrows	borrowing
break	깨뜨리다	breaks	breaking
bring	가져오다	brings	bringing
brush	닦다	brushes	brushing
build	세우다	builds	building
buy	사다	buys	buying
come	오다	comes	coming
cry	울다	cries	crying
cut	자르다	cuts	cutting
dance	춤추다	dances	dancing
die	죽다	dies	dying
do	하다	does	doing
eat	먹다	eats	eating
exercise	운동하다	exercises	exercising
fly	날다	flies	flying
go	가다	goes	going
lie	거짓말하다	lies	lying
make	만들다	makes	making
pass	건네주다	passes	passing
play	놀다	plays	playing
read	읽다	reads	reading
receive	받다	receives	receiving
run	달리다	runs	running
sit	앉다	sits	sitting

study	공부하다	studies	studying
swim	수영하다	swims	swimming
take	잡다	takes	taking
talk	말하다	talks	talking
teach	가르치다	teaches	teaching
tell	말하다	tells	telling
think	생각하다	thinks	thinking
throw	던지다	throws	throwing
wash	씻다	washes	washing
watch	보다	watches	watching
write	쓰다	writes	writing

2 진행형으로 쓸 수 없는 동사

감정, 소망, 감각, 지각, 가치나 소유를 나타내는 동사는 보통 진행형으로 쓰지 않는다.

be	~이다	hear	들리다	smell	~한 냄새가 나다
believe	믿다	know	알다	sound	~하게 들리다
care	관심을 갖다	like	좋아하다	taste	~한 맛이 나다
dislike	싫어하다	love	사랑하다	think	생각하다
find	찾다	need	필요하다	understand	이해하다
have	가지다	want	원하다	remember	기억하다
hate	싫어하다	see	보다	wish	바라다

3

동사의 현재형과 과거형

현재형		과거형
be	~이다, 있다	was / were
beat	치다	beat
become	되다	became
begin	시작하다	began
believe	믿다	believed
bite	물다	bit
blow	불다	blew
borrow	빌리다	borrowed
break	깨다	broke
bring	가져오다	brought
brush	이를 닦다	brushed
build	세우다	built
burn	타다	burned / burnt
buy	사다	bought
carry	들고 있다	carried
catch	잡다	caught
change	바꾸다	changed
choose	선택하다	chose
come	오다	came
cost	비용이 들다	cost
cut	자르다	cut
deal	다루다	dealt
dive	뛰어들다	dived / dove
do	하다	did
draw	그리다	drew

현재형		과거형
drink	마시다	drank
drive	운전하다	drove
eat	먹다	ate
fall	떨어지다	fell
feed	먹이다	fed
feel	느끼다	felt
fight	싸우다	fought
find	발견하다	found
fit	꼭 맞다	fit
fly	날다	flew
forget	잊다	forgot
forgive	용서하다	forgave
freeze	얼다	froze
get	얻다	got
give	주다	gave
go	가다	went
grow	자라다	grew
hang	걸다	hung
have	가지다	had
hear	듣다	heard
hide	숨기다	hid
hit	치다	hit
hold	쥐다	held
hurt	다치게 하다	hurt
keep	유지하다	kept

know	알다	knew
lay	놓다	laid
learn	배우다	learned / learnt
leave	떠나다	left
lend	빌려주다	lent
let	시키다	let
lie	눕다	lay
light	비추다	lit / lighted
lose	지다	lost
make	만들다	made
mean	의미하다	meant
meet	만나다	met
pay	지불하다	paid
put	놓다, 두다	put
read[ri:d]	읽다	read[red]
ride	타다	rode
ring	울리다	rang
rise	일어나다	rose
run	달리다	ran
say	말하다	said
see	보다	saw
sell	팔다	sold
send	보내다	sent
set	놓다	set
shake	흔들다	shook
shine	빛나다	shone
shoot	쏘다	shot
show	보여주다	showed
sing	노래하다	sang
sit	앉다	sat
sleep	자다	slept
slide	미끄러지다	slid
speak	말하다	spoke
spend	소비하다	spent
spread	펼치다	spread
stand	서 있다	stood
steal	훔치다	stole
strike	치다	struck
swear	맹세하다	swore
sweep	쓸다	swept
swim	수영하다	swam
swing	그네 타다	swung
take	잡다	took
teach	가르치다	taught
tear	찢다	tore
tell	말하다	told
think	생각하다	thought
throw	던지다	threw
understand	이해하다	understood
wake	깨우다	woke
wear	입다	wore
win	이기다	won
write	쓰다	wrote

지은이

NE능률 영어교육연구소

NE능률 영어교육연구소는 혁신적이며 효율적인 영어 교재를 개발하고
영어 학습의 질을 한 단계 높이고자 노력하는 NE능률의 연구조직입니다.

Grammar Bean 2

펴 낸 이 주민홍
펴 낸 곳 서울특별시 마포구 월드컵북로 396(상암동) 누리꿈스퀘어 비즈니스타워 10층
㈜NE능률 (우편번호 03925)
펴 낸 날 2019년 1월 5일 개정판 제1쇄 발행
2024년 7월 15일 제13쇄
전 화 02 2014 7114
팩 스 02 3142 0356
홈페이지 www.neungyule.com
등록번호 제1-68호
I S B N 979-11-253-2486-7 63740
정 가 12,000원

NE 능률

고객센터

교재 내용 문의 : contact.nebooks.co.kr (별도의 가입 절차 없이 작성 가능)
제품 구매, 교환, 불량, 반품 문의 : 02-2014-7114
☎ 전화문의는 본사 업무시간 중에만 가능합니다.

NE능률 교재 MAP

문법 구문 서술형

아래 교재 MAP을 참고하여 본인의 현재 혹은 목표 수준에 따라 교재를 선택하세요.
NE능률 교재들과 함께 영어실력을 쑥쑥~ 올려보세요!
MP3 등 교재 부가 학습 서비스 및 자세한 교재 정보는 www.nebooks.co.kr 에서 확인하세요.

초1-2

초3
- 그래머버디 1
- 초등영어 문법이 된다 Starter 1

초3-4
- 그래머버디 2
- 초등영어 문법이 된다 Starter 2
- 초등 Grammar Inside 1
- 초등 Grammar Inside 2

초4-5
- 그래머버디 3
- Grammar Bean 1
- Grammar Bean 2
- 초등영어 문법이 된다 1
- 초등 Grammar Inside 3
- 초등 Grammar Inside 4

초5-6
- Grammar Bean 3
- Grammar Bean 4
- 초등영어 문법이 된다 2
- 초등 Grammar Inside 5
- 초등 Grammar Inside 6

초6-예비중
- 능률중학영어 예비중
- Grammar Inside Starter
- 원리를 더한 영문법 STARTER

중1
- 능률중학영어 중1
- Grammar Zone 입문편
- Grammar Zone 워크북 입문편
- 1316 Grammar 1
- 문제로 마스터하는 중학영문법 1
- Grammar Inside 1
- 열중 16강 문법 1
- 쓰기로 마스터하는 중학서술형 1학년
- 중학 천문장 1

중1-2
- 능률중학영어 중2
- 1316 Grammar 2
- 문제로 마스터하는 중학영문법 2
- Grammar Inside 2
- 열중 16강 문법 2
- 원리를 더한 영문법 1
- 중학영문법 총정리 모의고사 1
- 중학 천문장 2

중2-3
- Grammar Zone 기초편
- Grammar Zone 워크북 기초편
- 1316 Grammar 3
- 원리를 더한 영문법 2
- 중학영문법 총정리 모의고사 2
- 쓰기로 마스터하는 중학서술형 2학년
- 중학 천문장 3

중3
- 능률중학영어 중3
- 문제로 마스터하는 중학영문법 3
- Grammar Inside 3
- 열중 16강 문법 3
- 중학영문법 총정리 모의고사 3
- 쓰기로 마스터하는 중학서술형 3학년

예비고-고1
- 문제로 마스터하는 고등영문법
- 올클 수능 어법 start
- 천문장 입문

고1
- Grammar Zone 기본편 1
- Grammar Zone 워크북 기본편 1
- Grammar Zone 기본편 2
- Grammar Zone 워크북 기본편 2
- 필히 통하는 고등 영문법 기본편
- 필히 통하는 고등 서술형 기본편
- 천문장 기본

고1-2
- 필히 통하는 고등 영문법 실력편
- 필히 통하는 고등 서술형 실전편
- TEPS BY STEP G+R Basic

고2-3
- Grammar Zone 종합편
- Grammar Zone 워크북 종합편
- 올클 수능 어법 완성
- 천문장 완성

고3

수능 이상/ 토플 80-89 · 텝스 600-699점
- TEPS BY STEP G+R 1

수능 이상/ 토플 90-99 · 텝스 700-799점
- TEPS BY STEP G+R 2

수능 이상/ 토플 100 · 텝스 800점 이상
- TEPS BY STEP G+R 3

GRAMMAR BEAN

그래머빈

2 Workbook

GRAMMAR BEAN

Workbook 2

CONTENTS

2권

UNIT 01 현재진행형

A (　　) 안에서 알맞은 것을 고르세요.

1 He (drinks / is drinking) water right now.

He (drinks / is drinking) three glasses of water a day.

2 I (talk / am talking) on the phone right now.

I (talk / am talking) on the phone every day.

3 My mom (cooks / is cooking) well.

My mom (cooks / is cooking) right now.

B 다음 문장을 현재진행형으로 바꿔 쓰세요.

1 We paint our house. → ______________________

2 Someone knocks on the door. → ______________________

3 People laugh with joy. → ______________________

4 I plant a tree in my garden. → ______________________

5 Two girls hold hands. → ______________________

6 Ben studies hard. → ______________________

7 She draws cats and dogs. → ______________________

8 Amy wears a big watch. → ______________________

Words **knock** 노크하다 **laugh** 웃다 **plant** 심다 **hold hands** 손을 잡다 **draw** 그리다

C 보기에서 알맞은 말을 골라 빈칸에 쓰세요.

[보기] isn't aren't am not don't doesn't

1 They ________ eating a cake.

2 Hara ________ baking cookies.

3 Mike ________ help his mom.

4 I ________ carrying an umbrella.

5 Kelly ________ staying at home.

6 You ________ study hard.

D 우리말과 같은 뜻이 되도록 ( ) 안에서 알맞은 것을 고르세요.

1 내가 너무 빨리 말하고 있니? → (Am / Do) I talking too fast?

2 그 새는 높이 나니? → (Is / Does) the bird fly high?

3 학생들이 떠들고 있니? → (Are / Do) the students chatting?

4 너 지금 공을 던지고 있니? → (Are / Do) you throwing the ball now?

5 Cathy는 의자에 앉아 있니? → (Is / Does) Cathy sitting on a chair?

6 너는 매일 책을 읽니? → (Are / Do) you read books every day?

Words **bake** 굽다 **carry** 들고 있다 **chat** 수다를 떨다 **throw** 던지다

UNIT 02 be동사의 과거형

A

(　) 안에서 알맞은 것을 고르세요.

1 The mountain (was / were) very high.

2 The pictures (was / were) beautiful.

3 You and I (was / were) good friends.

4 (Are / Were) you at home now?

5 The tree (is / was) small last year.

6 The men (are / were) very kind yesterday.

7 The sky (is / was) clear last week.

B

빈칸에 알맞은 be동사의 과거형을 쓰세요.

1 Allen ________ very kind to me.

2 The boy ________ a liar.

3 The answer ________ wrong.

4 We ________ very hungry.

5 Two pencils ________ in the box.

6 They ________ happy at the party.

7 I ________ on a basketball team.

Words **clear** 맑은 **liar** 거짓말쟁이 **wrong** 틀린

C

빈칸에 공통으로 들어갈 말을 쓰세요.

1 • We ________ very tired.
  • You ________ brave last night.

2 • The weather ________ nice yesterday.
  • Kevin ________ my classmate.

3 • There ________ lots of people in the park.
  • My brother and I ________ in Canada last month.

4 • I ________ a big fan of baseball.
  • Nancy ________ very busy last week.

D

우리말과 같은 뜻이 되도록 빈칸에 알맞은 말을 쓰세요.

1 바닥은 깨끗하지 않았다. → The floor ________ clean.

2 그들의 가방들은 무거웠니? → ________ their bags heavy?

3 나는 피곤하지 않았다. → I ________ tired.

4 그들은 유명한 배우였니? → ________ they famous actors?

5 그 우유는 차가웠다. → The milk ________ cold.

6 그 영화는 좋았니? → ________ the movie good?

7 동물원에 많은 사람들이 있었다. → There ________ a lot of people at the zoo.

Words **brave** 용감한 **floor** 바닥 **heavy** 무거운 **famous** 유명한

Grammar Test

[1-5] 보기와 같이 질문에 알맞은 대답을 쓰세요.

[보기] A: Is she looking for her cat?
B: Yes, she is. / No, she isn't.

1 A: Are you making spaghetti now?
B: Yes, ________. / No, ________.

2 A: Was your brother watching a movie?
B: Yes, ________. / No, ________.

3 A: Were there children on the playground?
B: Yes, ________. / No, ________.

4 A: Is Jenny singing a song?
B: Yes, ________. / No, ________.

5 A: Am I eating too much?
B: Yes, ________. / No, ________.

[6-9] 주어진 단어를 이용하여 과거시제의 의문문을 완성하세요.

6 ________ your son ________ that day? (sick)

7 ________ you ________ for school yesterday? (late)

8 ________ he ________ last weekend? (busy)

9 ________ they ________ ten years ago? (poor)

Words **look for** ~을 찾다 **spaghetti** 스파게티 **playground** 놀이터 **be late for** ~에 늦다

[10-15] 다음 문장의 동사를 과거형으로 바꿔 쓰세요.

10 The students are very diligent.

→ ______________________________

11 The soup is warm.

→ ______________________________

12 My parents are bakers.

→ ______________________________

13 Is there a problem with your phone?

→ ______________________________

14 I am at the bookstore in the mall.

→ ______________________________

15 There are too many people in the building.

→ ______________________________

[16-20] 밑줄 친 부분을 바르게 고쳐 쓰세요.

16 Are you <u>study</u> in the library now? → __________

17 I <u>not am</u> drinking mango juice. → __________

18 We <u>is</u> dancing on the stage. → __________

19 <u>Are</u> you tired last night? → __________

20 He <u>weren't</u> angry about my mistake. → __________

Words **diligent** 부지런한 **warm** 따뜻한 **baker** 제빵사 **problem** 문제 **building** 건물 **library** 도서관 **stage** 무대

UNIT 03 일반동사의 과거형

A ( ) 안에서 알맞은 것을 고르세요.

1 I (do / was) the laundry every Saturday.

2 The show (starts / started) 10 minutes ago.

3 He (reads / read) the book last year.

4 I (meet / met) him in 2009.

5 I (go / am going) to school by bus every morning.

6 She (tries / tried) it a month ago.

7 I (watch / watched) TV news last night.

B 우리말과 같은 뜻이 되도록 빈칸에 알맞은 말을 쓰세요.

1 Bill은 그 학교를 방문했다. → Bill ________ the school.

2 그는 장미꽃 열 송이를 샀다. → He ________ ten roses.

3 Amy는 빨간색 모자를 썼다. → Amy ________ a red cap.

4 그들은 노래 두 곡을 불렀다. → They ________ two songs.

5 Jenny는 편지를 한 통 썼다. → Jenny ________ a letter.

6 나는 피자 세 조각을 먹었다. → I ________ three pieces of pizza.

7 우리는 어제 공원에 갔다. → We ________ to the park yesterday.

Words **do the laundry** 빨래를 하다 **ago** ~ 전에 **cap** 모자 **piece** 조각

C 보기에서 알맞은 동사를 골라 과거형으로 바꾸어 문장을 완성하세요.

[보기] wear give eat start find break

1 She ________ a white skirt yesterday.

2 The movie ________ 30 minutes ago.

3 Tiffany ________ spaghetti for lunch.

4 Mom ________ a beautiful necklace to me.

5 They played baseball and ________ a window.

6 I ________ the key under the bed.

D 밑줄 친 부분이 맞으면 O, 틀리면 바르게 고쳐 쓰세요.

1 She <u>rides</u> a bike yesterday afternoon. → ____________

2 They <u>meet</u> at a party a month ago. → ____________

3 Jessica <u>goes</u> to the library last Saturday. → ____________

4 We <u>visited</u> our grandparents last weekend. → ____________

5 My parents <u>marry</u> in 1995. → ____________

6 She usually <u>has</u> breakfast at 8. → ____________

7 Jerry <u>sleep</u> for only two hours last night. → ____________

Words **spaghetti** 스파게티 **necklace** 목걸이 **window** 창문 **library** 도서관 **marry** 결혼하다 **usually** 보통, 대개

UNIT 04 일반동사 과거형의 부정문과 의문문

A 우리말과 같은 뜻이 되도록 보기의 단어를 이용하여 문장을 완성하세요.

[보기] find drink buy go lose

1 Mark가 그 우유를 마셨니?
→ ________ Mark ________ the milk?

2 너는 그녀의 전화번호를 알아냈니?
→ ________ you ________ her phone number?

3 그들은 그 식당에 갔니?
→ ________ ________ ________ to the restaurant?

4 너는 이 음악 파일들을 샀니?
→ ________ ________ ________ these music files?

5 그녀는 가방을 잃어버렸니?
→ ________ ________ ________ her bag?

B 다음 문장을 부정문으로 바꿔 쓰세요.

1 I had black coffee. → ____________________

2 He made new friends. → ____________________

3 They cried yesterday. → ____________________

4 I watched the movie yesterday. → ____________________

5 She called you last night. → ____________________

Words **find** 알아내다 **lose** 잃어버리다

C 빈칸에 알맞은 대답을 쓰세요.

1 A: Did you feed the dog?

B: ________, ________ ________. I forgot.

2 A: Did you go out last night?

B: ________, ________ ________. I went to see a movie.

3 A: Did he have cereal this morning?

B: ________, ________ ________. He had a sandwich.

4 A: Did Tony change his hairstyle?

B: ________, ________ ________. I like his new hairstyle.

5 A: Did she take the bus?

B: ________, ________ ________. She took the train.

D 밑줄 친 부분을 바르게 고쳐 쓰세요.

1 Did you lived in Chicago last year? → ________________

2 She sends an e-mail an hour ago. → ________________

3 I don't said anything to him yesterday. → ________________

4 He didn't went to school yesterday. → ________________

5 Do you study last night? → ________________

6 Mom meeted my teacher last week. → ________________

Words **feed** 먹이다 **cereal** 시리얼 **anything** 아무것도

Grammar Test

[1-6] **다음 문장을 과거시제로 바꿔 쓰세요.**

1 I go to the zoo with my friends.

→ ______________________________

2 Do you have a watch?

→ ______________________________

3 He doesn't tell the secret.

→ ______________________________

4 Suji breaks the window.

→ ______________________________

5 They win the game.

→ ______________________________

6 Does the girl turn on the TV?

→ ______________________________

[7-10] **주어진 단어를 이용하여 과거시제의 의문문을 완성하세요.**

7 ________ you ________ my cap? (wear)

8 ________ they ________ Jack's house? (visit)

9 ________ she ________ a rest yesterday? (take)

10 ________ Jimmy ________ his room last Saturday? (clean)

Words **secret** 비밀 **break** 깨다, 부수다 **win** 이기다 **turn on** ~을 켜다 **wear** 입다, 쓰다 **visit** 방문하다 **take a rest** 쉬다, 휴식하다 **clean** 청소하다

[11-16] **우리말과 같은 뜻이 되도록 주어진 말을 이용하여 문장을 만드세요.**

11 아빠가 마당에 나무 한 그루를 심었다. (plant a tree)

→ My father ______________________ in the yard.

12 우리 반은 수요일에 수학 시험을 봤다. (take a math test)

→ Our class ______________________ on Wednesday.

13 너는 어제 교복을 입었니? (wear your school uniform)

→ ______________________ yesterday?

14 그들은 그 책을 읽지 않았다. (read the book)

→ ______________________

15 Jennifer는 지난 주말에 집에서 머물렀다. (stay at home)

→ ______________________ last weekend.

16 우리들은 지난밤에 공포 영화를 보지 않았다. (watch a horror movie)

→ ______________________ last night.

17 **대화가 어색한 것을 고르세요.**

① A: Did you get an A on the math exam?
B: No, I didn't. I got a B.

② A: Did you see a doctor yesterday?
B: Yes, I did. I had a stomachache.

③ A: Did you sleep well last night?
B: Yes, I did. It was noisy outside.

④ A: I didn't go to school today.
B: Did you tell your mother?

Words **plant** 심다 **yard** 마당 **school uniform** 교복 **read** 읽다 **stay** 머무르다 **stomachache** 복통 **noisy** 시끄러운

[18-19] 올바른 문장을 고르세요.

18 ① She had dinner with her family.
② Do you wrote the novel?
③ He didn't wakes up early today.
④ Emily drew a picture right now.

19 ① I sent five e-mails tomorrow.
② Did Olivia lost the key?
③ I didn't knew him well before.
④ My brother read a comic book yesterday.

[20-21] 틀린 문장을 고르세요.

20 ① I swam in the river yesterday.
② Did he played the piano?
③ My father didn't wash his car.
④ Did you teach science before?

21 ① Did you call me in the morning?
② I didn't do my homework.
③ They lived in China last year.
④ Sam and his brother fight an hour ago.

Words **novel** 소설 **early** 일찍 **key** 열쇠 **river** 강 **teach** 가르치다 **science** 과학

[22-24] 질문에 대한 대답으로 알맞은 것을 모두 고르세요. (2개)

22

A: Did you cook the meal?

B: ______________________________

① Yes. I didn't cook the meal.

② Yes, I did. Do you like it?

③ No, I didn't. Mr. Johnson cooked it.

④ No, I wasn't. I wasn't a good cook.

23

A: Did she go to the concert last night?

B: ______________________________

① Yes. She didn't have time.

② No. She took a rest at home.

③ No, she didn't. The singer is her favorite.

④ Yes, she did. She likes the singer very much.

24

A: Did the children have a party on Sunday?

B: ______________________________

① Yes. It was Laura's birthday.

② Yes, they did. I'm going to the party now.

③ No, they didn't. They had a great time.

④ No. They go to the museum on weekends.

Words meal 식사 concert 콘서트 museum 박물관

UNIT 05 형용사

A 다음 형용사의 반의어를 고르세요.

1	new	☐ low	☐ old	☐ lazy
2	bad	☐ good	☐ hot	☐ unhappy
3	slow	☐ fast	☐ small	☐ sad
4	high	☐ angry	☐ low	☐ fast
5	expensive	☐ cheap	☐ poor	☐ long
6	rich	☐ unkind	☐ poor	☐ low
7	clean	☐ dirty	☐ new	☐ windy

B 주어진 단어를 바르게 배열하여 문장을 완성하세요.

1 He is (great / a / teacher). → ____________________

2 I like (juice / this / cold). → ____________________

3 (boy / little / the) is my brother. → ____________________

4 (computer / your / new) is great. → ____________________

5 (building / tall / the) is famous. → ____________________

6 I'm (girl / a / smart). → ____________________

7 He likes (expensive / his / watch). → ____________________

8 I have (umbrella / yellow / a). → ____________________

Words **low** 낮은 **unkind** 불친절한 **clean** 깨끗한 **windy** 바람이 부는 **famous** 유명한 **umbrella** 우산

C 우리말과 같은 뜻이 되도록 주어진 단어를 이용하여 문장을 완성하세요.

1 그들은 행복하다. (happy)
→ They ________ ________.

2 나는 빨간 드레스 한 벌을 가지고 있다. (red)
→ I have ________ ________ dress.

3 저 키 큰 소년은 나의 친구이다. (tall)
→ ________ ________ boy is my friend.

4 그녀는 이 갈색 고양이를 좋아한다. (brown)
→ She likes ________ ________ cat.

5 나는 그의 슬픈 이야기를 안다. (sad)
→ I know ________ ________ story.

6 이 큰 안경은 나의 것이 아니다. (big)
→ ________ ________ glasses aren't mine.

7 큰 나무 두 그루가 있다. (large)
→ There are ________ ________ trees.

D 밑줄 친 부분을 바르게 고쳐 쓰세요.

1 I like new my computer. → ________________

2 The bag pink is mine. → ________________

3 She is wise a girl. → ________________

4 Your voice wonderful is. → ________________

5 We hungry are now. → ________________

6 There is bright a star in the sky. → ________________

7 This girl is a my girlfriend. → ________________

Words **story** 이야기 **wise** 지혜로운 **wonderful** 훌륭한, 멋진 **bright** 빛나는

UNIT 06 지시형용사, 수량형용사

A (　　) 안에서 알맞은 것을 고르세요.

1 There isn't (many / much) air in this room.

2 I have (a little / a few) questions.

3 I like (this / these) cookies.

4 You have (few / little) time.

5 (This / These) music is beautiful.

6 She needs (a few / a little) money.

7 I know (many / much) interesting stories.

8 There's (few / little) water in some countries.

B 우리말과 같은 뜻이 되도록 빈칸에 알맞은 말을 쓰세요.

1 나는 저 그림이 좋다. → I like ______________ picture.

2 이 배우는 유명하다. → ______________ actor is famous.

3 저 토끼들은 귀엽다. → ______________ rabbits are cute.

4 나는 이 빨간 꽃들을 좋아한다. → I like ______________ red flowers.

5 그는 시계를 몇 개 가지고 있다. → He has ______________ watches.

6 그들은 희망이 거의 없다. → They have ______________ hope.

7 그녀는 많은 이메일을 쓴다. → She writes ______________ e-mails.

8 공원에는 사람이 거의 없다. → There are ______________ people in the park.

Words **air** 공기 **interesting** 흥미로운 **country** 나라 **hope** 희망

C 밑줄 친 부분을 바르게 고쳐 쓰세요.

1 I have <u>much</u> games on my cell phone. → ____________

2 She watches <u>little</u> TV shows. → ____________

3 <u>These</u> movie is very sad. → ____________

4 There isn't <u>many</u> hot water. → ____________

5 <u>That</u> potatoes are small. → ____________

6 There's <u>few</u> Coke in the glass. → ____________

7 I want <u>a few</u> water. → ____________

8 They have <u>much</u> books. → ____________

D 우리말과 같은 뜻이 되도록 주어진 말을 바르게 배열하세요.

1 도로에 많은 버스들이 있다. (buses)

→ There are ____________________ on the street.

2 그는 노란색 셔츠가 거의 없다. (yellow shirts).

→ He has ____________________.

3 이 작은 아이들은 똑똑하다. (little children)

→ ____________________ are smart.

4 저 키 큰 남자들은 독일에서 왔다. (tall men)

→ ____________________ are from Germany.

5 나는 몇 개의 새 펜들이 필요하다. (new pens).

→ I need ____________________.

6 이 배구공들은 나의 것이다. (volleyballs)

→ ____________________ are mine.

Words **street** 도로, 거리 **Germany** 독일 **volleyball** 배구공

Grammar Test

[1-4] **보기와 같이 질문에 알맞은 대답을 쓰세요.**

> [보기] A: Is he tall?
> B: No, he isn't. He's short.

1 A: Is the bag big?
B: No, it isn't. ____________________.

2 A: Is this cheap?
B: No, it isn't. ____________________.

3 A: Is your room clean?
B: No, it isn't. ____________________.

4 A: Is the coffee hot?
B: No, it isn't. ____________________.

[5-11] **밑줄 친 부분이 맞으면 O, 틀리면 바르게 고쳐 쓰세요.**

5 You have socks cute. → ______________

6 There are a little cats in the park. → ______________

7 My shirt is a long. → ______________

8 There are much songs in the album. → ______________

9 His cap is small. → ______________

10 There are tall many trees. → ______________

11 There's few milk in the bottle. → ______________

Words **socks** 양말 **bottle** 병

[12-17] **우리말과 같은 뜻이 되도록 보기에서 알맞은 말을 골라 빈칸에 쓰세요.**

[보기] little a little few a few much many

12 그는 친구가 많다.

→ He has ____________ friends.

13 그 가게에는 인형이 거의 없다.

→ There are ____________ dolls in the store.

14 그들은 피아노를 몇 대 가지고 있다.

→ They have ____________ pianos.

15 그는 건강에 관심이 거의 없다.

→ He has ____________ interest in health.

16 나는 지갑에 돈이 조금 있다.

→ I have ____________ money in my wallet.

17 나는 오늘 시간이 많지 않다.

→ I don't have ____________ time today.

[18-19] **보기와 같이 문장을 만드세요.**

[보기] She's a singer. She is amazing.
→ She's an amazing singer.

18 This is a book. It's interesting.

→ ______________________________

19 They're lawyers. They're famous.

→ ______________________________

Words **doll** 인형 **interest** 관심 **health** 건강 **wallet** 지갑 **amazing** 놀라운 **lawyer** 변호사

[20-25] **우리말과 같은 뜻이 되도록 주어진 말을 이용하여 문장을 완성하세요.**

20 그는 재미있는 잡지 한 권을 가지고 있다. (magazine, fun)

→ He has ______________________________.

21 나는 이 맛있는 요구르트를 매일 먹는다. (yogurt, delicious)

→ I eat ______________________________ every day.

22 그들은 돈이 거의 없다. (money)

→ They have ______________________________.

23 나는 새 카메라 하나를 원한다. (camera, new)

→ I want ______________________________.

24 나는 몇 개의 따뜻한 담요가 필요하다. (blanket, warm)

→ I need ______________________________.

25 나는 저녁에 뜨거운 물 몇 잔을 마신다. (cup, water, hot)

→ I drink ______________________________ in the evening.

[26-27] **틀린 문장을 고르세요.**

26
① She has big eyes.
② He has brown a dog.
③ They always eat a lot for dinner.
④ There is little water in the river.

27
① The Coke is very cold.
② I need a soft pillow.
③ That movie is very funny.
④ This is a my computer.

Words **magazine** 잡지 **yogurt** 요구르트 **delicious** 맛있는 **blanket** 담요 **warm** 따뜻한 **soft** 부드러운 **pillow** 베개

28 밑줄 친 부분의 쓰임이 다른 하나를 고르세요.

① Is this your car?
② This song is very good.
③ I like this book.
④ Try this dress on.

[29-32] 빈칸에 알맞은 것을 모두 고르세요. (2개)

29

Jessica is _________.

① tall ② singer
③ an artist ④ a pretty

30

This is a _________ comic book.

① my ② new
③ few ④ good

31

There are _________ bikes on the road.

① a ② a few
③ a little ④ a lot of

32

There isn't _________ coffee in the cup.

① much ② many
③ little ④ a lot of

Words try on ~을 입어보다 road 도로

UNIT 07 who, what

A 우리말과 같은 뜻이 되도록 빈칸에 알맞은 의문사를 쓰세요.

1 이것은 누구의 지갑이니?
→ ________ wallet is this?

2 누가 이 일을 했니?
→ ________ did this work?

3 그녀는 무엇을 요리하고 있니?
→ ________ is she cooking?

4 그는 누구를 싫어하니?
→ ________ does he dislike?

5 너는 어떤 노래를 좋아하니?
→ ________ songs do you like?

6 저 잘생긴 신사는 누구니?
→ ________ is that handsome gentleman?

B 보기에서 알맞은 대답을 골라 쓰세요.

[보기] ⓐ She is my aunt. ⓑ I went hiking.
ⓒ I helped old people. ⓓ It's my father's.

1 Who is that woman? ______

2 Whose camera is this? ______

3 What did you do last Sunday? ______

4 Who did you help? ______

Words **dislike** 싫어하다 **handsome** 잘생긴 **gentleman** 신사

C 밑줄 친 부분을 묻는 의문문으로 바꿔 쓰세요.

1 Ms. Morrison is my science teacher.
→ ______

2 I'm looking at James.
→ ______

3 It is my book.
→ ______

4 I'm listening to rock music.
→ ______

5 Amy is making pasta.
→ ______

D 우리말과 같은 뜻이 되도록 주어진 말을 바르게 배열하세요.

1 누가 어젯밤에 창문을 열었니? (last night / the window / who / opened)
→ ______

2 저것들은 누구의 가방이니? (those / bags / are / whose)
→ ______

3 너는 무엇을 읽고 있니? (are / what / reading / you)
→ ______

4 누가 너의 반 친구였니? (was / your / who / classmate)
→ ______

5 어느 동물을 가장 좋아하니? (what / animal / like / most / do / you)
→ ______

Words **science** 과학 **classmate** 반 친구

UNIT 08 where, when, why

A 보기에서 알맞은 의문사를 골라 빈칸에 쓰세요.

[보기] what when where why

1 __________ did you graduate from high school?
– Last year.

2 __________ were you looking for me?
– Because I needed your help.

3 __________ did you get this medicine?
– I bought it from the drugstore.

4 __________ is your favorite food?
– I love potato salad.

5 __________ are you from?
– I'm from Canada.

6 __________ did she buy the shoes?
– At a department store.

7 __________ is he wearing?
– He's wearing a Superman costume.

8 __________ does she look so sad?
– She failed the exam.

9 __________ does the basketball game start?
– At 2:00 p.m.

Words **graduate** 졸업하다 **medicine** 약 **drugstore** 약국 **department store** 백화점 **costume** 의상 **fail** 실패하다, (시험에) 떨어지다

B 보기에서 알맞은 대답을 골라 쓰세요.

[보기]
ⓐ I caught a cold.
ⓑ I visited some famous museums.
ⓒ It starts at 7:00.
ⓓ She is in Japan.
ⓔ She ate a piece of pizza.

1 Where is your daughter? ______

2 When does the game start? ______

3 Why did you go to the hospital? ______

4 Where did you go in London? ______

5 What did she eat last night? ______

C 밑줄 친 부분을 바르게 고쳐 쓰세요.

1 Why she is poor? → ______________

2 When did your father married? → ______________

3 When do you sad? → ______________

4 Where are you work? → ______________

5 Why was he lie to you? → ______________

6 When does she goes to the pool? → ______________

7 When are your birthday? → ______________

Words **catch a cold** 감기에 걸리다 **museum** 박물관 **marry** 결혼하다 **pool** 수영장

UNIT 09 how

A 보기에서 알맞은 말을 골라 빈칸에 쓰세요.

[보기]	How	How old	How long	How often
	How tall	How many	How much	How far

1 A: ____________ did you wait?

B: For an hour.

2 A: ____________ does she look?

B: She looks tired.

3 A: ____________ countries did you travel to?

B: I traveled to seven countries.

4 A: ____________ is the police station from here?

B: It's about 1 km away.

5 A: ____________ is that hat?

B: It's 10 dollars.

6 A: ____________ do you go dancing?

B: Once a month.

7 A: ____________ are you?

B: I'm 12 years old.

8 A: ____________ time do you need?

B: I need two hours.

9 A: ____________ is Seoul Tower?

B: It's over 200 m.

Words **wait** 기다리다 **look** 보이다 **travel** 여행하다 **police station** 경찰서

B 밑줄 친 부분이 맞으면 O, 틀리면 바르게 고쳐 쓰세요.

1 How much students are there on the bus? → ________

2 How old are your teacher? → ________

3 How many friends did you invite? → ________

4 How tall does that mountain? → ________

5 How much people live in this town? → ________

6 How much salt are in the sea? → ________

7 How many oranges is there in the basket? → ________

8 How were you hear the news? → ________

C 우리말과 같은 뜻이 되도록 주어진 말을 이용하여 문장을 만드세요.

1 너는 어떻게 그것을 알았니? (how, know that)

→ ________________________________

2 얼마나 많은 우유를 마셨니? (how much milk, drink)

→ ________________________________

3 너는 몇 개의 동전을 가지고 있니? (how many coins, have)

→ ________________________________

4 너는 어떻게 답을 알아냈니? (how, find the answer)

→ ________________________________

5 얼마나 많은 박물관을 그녀가 방문했었니? (how many museums, visit)

→ ________________________________

6 얼마만큼의 설탕이 필요하니? (how much sugar, need)

→ ________________________________

Words **invite** 초대하다 **town** 마을 **basket** 바구니 **coin** 동전 **find** 알아내다 **answer** 답

Grammar Test

[1-6] 보기에서 알맞은 의문사를 골라 쓰세요.

[보기] when who how why where

1 A: ________ much water do you drink?
B: One bottle a day.

2 A: ________ are you wearing a cap?
B: Because I didn't wash my hair.

3 A: ________ will you hand in the report?
B: Tomorrow morning.

4 A: ________ do you know Jim?
B: Jenny introduced him to me yesterday.

5 A: ________ were you?
B: I was at home.

6 A: ________ is there?
B: It's Mike.

[7-10] 밑줄 친 부분을 바르게 고쳐 쓰세요.

7 Why you called me? → ________________

8 How many money do you need? → ________________

9 Whom gave you this present? → ________________

10 When does your birthday? → ________________

Words **hand in** 제출하다 **report** 보고서 **introduce** 소개하다 **present** 선물

[11-17] B의 대답을 보고 A의 질문을 만드세요.

11 A: ______________________

B: He came back last month.

12 A: ______________________

B: It's twenty dollars.

13 A: ______________________

B: It'll take one hour.

14 A: ______________________

B: She's in the kitchen.

15 A: ______________________

B: I'm ten years old.

16 A: ______________________

B: I like purple.

17 A: ______________________

B: I got up at 7 o'clock.

[18-20] 보기에서 알맞은 대답을 골라 쓰세요.

[보기] ⓐ It was on the sofa.
ⓑ Because I finished my work early.
ⓒ It's 8,848 meters high.

18 Why did you come home early? ________

19 How high is Mt. Everest? ________

20 Where did you find the key? ________

Words purple 자주색의

[21-27] **우리말과 같은 뜻이 되도록 주어진 말을 이용하여 문장을 만드세요.**

21 너는 언제 졸업을 하니? (graduate)

→ ______________________________

22 너는 누구에게 이야기를 하고 있니? (talk to)

→ ______________________________

23 너는 어떻게 그녀를 만났니? (meet her)

→ ______________________________

24 너는 얼마나 자주 너의 컴퓨터를 업데이트 하니? (update your computer)

→ ______________________________

25 너는 너의 휴대전화를 언제 샀니? (buy your cell phone)

→ ______________________________

26 너는 그 음악을 어디에서 다운로드 했니? (download the song)

→ ______________________________

27 누가 이 사진을 찍었니? (take this picture)

→ ______________________________

28 **대화가 어색한 것을 고르세요.**

① A: How much are these pants?
B: They're 100 dollars.

② A: Where are you going?
B: I'm going to the airport.

③ A: Why do you need a car?
B: I need it next weekend.

④ A: When can you finish this work?
B: Sorry, but I'm not sure.

Words **graduate** 졸업하다 **update** 업데이트 하다 **download** 다운로드 하다 **airport** 공항 **weekend** 주말

[29-30] 질문에 대한 대답으로 알맞은 것을 모두 고르세요. (2개)

29

A: What do you do in your free time?

B: ________________________________

① I meet my friends.

② I'll go see a movie.

③ I usually play computer games.

④ I'm watching TV now.

30

A: Where can I meet them?

B: ________________________________

① At the shop on Main Street.

② Yes, you can. Hurry up!

③ No, I don't know. Sorry.

④ Go to their office.

[31-32] 틀린 문장을 고르세요.

31

① Whose phone is this?

② How old are you?

③ What are you going to do?

④ Whom changed the password?

32

① Why did you waited for me?

② How much is the dress?

③ What is he wearing now?

④ What time does the movie start?

Words hurry up 서두르다 password 암호

UNIT 10 비인칭 주어 it

A 우리말을 영어로 바르게 옮긴 것은 O, 그렇지 않은 것은 바르게 고쳐 쓰세요.

1 오늘 날씨가 화창하다.
This is sunny today. → __________________

2 5월 3일이다.
It's May 3. → __________________

3 한국은 여름이다.
This is summer in Korea. → __________________

4 오늘은 바람이 몹시 분다.
It's very windy today. → __________________

5 4시 15분이다.
This is four fifteen. → __________________

B 대화의 빈칸에 알맞은 말을 쓰세요.

1 A: What's the ________ today?
B: ________ January 18.

2 A: What ________ is ________?
B: ________ Tuesday.

3 A: Can I go home now?
B: ________ seven thirty now. You can go at eight.

4 A: How can we get there? By train?
B: No, ________ really far to Canada. We'll go there by plane.

Words **sunny** 화창한 **windy** 바람이 부는

C 우리말과 같은 뜻이 되도록 빈칸에 알맞은 말을 쓰세요.

1 오늘이 화요일이니, 수요일이니?
→ Is ________ Tuesday or Wednesday?

2 오스트레일리아는 따뜻하다.
→ ________ is warm in Australia.

3 지금 시각은 2시 45분이다.
→ ________ ________ two forty-five now.

4 오늘은 2월 25일이다.
→ ________ is February 25 today.

5 집에서 아빠 사무실까지는 10킬로미터이다.
→ ________ ________ 10 km from my home to my father's office.

D 주어진 말을 바르게 배열하여 문장을 만드세요.

1 (is / cold / it / today)
→ ______________________________

2 (all day long / rained / it)
→ ______________________________

3 (5 o'clock / is / in / it / the morning)
→ ______________________________

4 (from here / to the national park / 40 miles / it's)
→ ______________________________

Words **Australia** 오스트레일리아 **office** 사무실 **the national park** 국립공원

Grammar Test

[1-6] B의 대답을 보고 A의 질문을 완성하세요.

1 A: ________ ________ ________ ________ now?
B: It's eight ten.

2 A: ________ ________ ________ ________ from here to Seoul?
B: It's one kilometer.

3 A: ________ ________ the weather?
B: It's rainy and windy.

4 A: ________ ________ ________ ________ today?
B: It's Sunday.

5 A: ________ ________ ________ today?
B: It's May 2.

6 A: ________ ________ is it?
B: It's summer.

[7-12] 밑줄 친 부분을 바르게 고쳐 쓰세요.

7 <u>This is</u> seven thirty now. → ____________ seven thirty now.

8 <u>What day was it</u> today? → ____________ today?

9 What time is <u>that</u>? → What time is ____________?

10 <u>There is</u> not far from here. → ____________ not far from here.

11 <u>How</u> is the weather like? → ____________ is the weather like?

12 <u>Now</u> is June 19 today. → ____________ is June 19 today.

Words **weather** 날씨

13 대화가 어색한 것을 고르세요.

① A: It's too hot.
B: Open the window.

② A: What season is it?
B: It's June.

③ A: When is your birthday?
B: My birthday is March 1.

④ A: What time is it now?
B: It's ten.

14 밑줄 친 부분의 쓰임이 다른 하나를 고르세요.

① It's very expensive.

② It's foggy and cold.

③ It's already eight thirty.

④ It's too far from here.

15 질문에 대한 대답으로 올 수 있는 것을 모두 고르세요. (2개)

A: What will the weather be like tomorrow?
B: ______________________

① It was cloudy all day.

② Yes, I know. It'll be sunny.

③ It's going to snow.

④ It'll be warm but windy.

Words **season** 계절 **expensive** 비싼 **foggy** 안개가 낀 **cloudy** 흐린

UNIT 01 현재진행형

A 1 is drinking, drinks 2 am talking, talk
3 cooks, is cooking

B 1 We are painting our house.
2 Someone is knocking on the door.
3 People are laughing with joy.
4 I am planting a tree in my garden.
5 Two girls are holding hands.
6 Ben is studying hard.
7 She is drawing cats and dogs.
8 Amy is wearing a big watch.

C 1 aren't 2 isn't 3 doesn't 4 am not
5 isn't 6 don't

D 1 Am 2 Does 3 Are 4 Are 5 Is 6 Do

UNIT 02 be동사의 과거형

A 1 was 2 were 3 were 4 Are 5 was
6 were 7 was

B 1 was 2 was 3 was 4 were 5 were
6 were 7 was

C 1 were 2 was 3 were 4 was

D 1 wasn't 2 Were 3 wasn't 4 Were 5 was
6 Was 7 were

Grammar Test ▸▸Unit 1~2

1 I am / I'm not 2 he was / he wasn't
3 there were / there weren't
4 she is / she isn't 5 you are / you aren't
6 Was, sick 7 Were, late 8 Was, busy
9 Were, poor
10 The students were very diligent.
11 The soup was warm.
12 My parents were bakers.
13 Was there a problem with your phone?
14 I was at the bookstore in the mall.
15 There were too many people in the building. 16 studying 17 am not 18 are
19 Were 20 wasn't[was not]

UNIT 03 일반동사의 과거형

A 1 do 2 started 3 read 4 met 5 go
6 tried 7 watched

B 1 visited 2 bought 3 wore 4 sang
5 wrote 6 ate[had] 7 went

C 1 wore 2 started 3 ate 4 gave 5 broke
6 found

D 1 rode 2 met 3 went 4 O 5 married
6 O 7 slept

UNIT 04 일반동사 과거형의 부정문과 의문문

A 1 Did, drink 2 Did, find 3 Did they go
4 Did you buy 5 Did she lose

B 1 I didn't like black coffee.
2 He didn't make new friends.
3 They didn't cry yesterday.
4 I didn't watch the movie yesterday.
5 She didn't call you last night.

C 1 No, I didn't 2 Yes, I did 3 No, he didn't
4 Yes, he did 5 No, she didn't

D 1 Did you live 2 sent 3 didn't say 4 go
5 Did you study 6 met

Grammar Test ▸▸Unit 3~4

1 I went to the zoo with my friends.
2 Did you have a watch?
3 He didn't[did not] tell the secret.
4 Suji broke the window.
5 They won the game.
6 Did the girl turn on the TV? 7 Did, wear
8 Did, visit 9 Did, take 10 Did, clean
11 planted a tree 12 took a math test
13 Did you wear your school uniform
14 They didn't[did not] read the book.
15 Jennifer stayed at home
16 We didn't[did not] watch a horror movie
17 ③ 18 ① 19 ④ 20 ② 21 ④ 22 ②, ③
23 ②, ④ 24 ①, ④

UNIT 05 형용사

A 1 old 2 good 3 fast 4 low 5 cheap
6 poor 7 dirty
B 1 He is a great teacher.
2 I like this cold juice.
3 The little boy is my brother.
4 Your new computer is great.
5 The tall building is famous.
6 I'm a smart girl.
7 He likes his expensive watch.
8 I have a yellow umbrella.
C 1 are happy 2 a[one] red 3 That tall
4 this brown 5 his sad 6 These big
7 two large
D 1 my new computer 2 The pink bag
3 a wise girl 4 is wonderful
5 are hungry 6 a bright star
7 my girlfriend

UNIT 06 지시형용사, 수량형용사

A 1 much 2 a few 3 these 4 little 5 This
6 a little 7 many 8 little
B 1 that 2 This 3 Those 4 these 5 a few
6 little 7 many[a lot of] 8 few
C 1 many[a lot of] 2 few 3 This
4 much[a lot of] 5 Those 6 little
7 a little 8 many[a lot of]
D 1 many[a lot of] buses
2 few yellow shirts 3 These little children
4 Those tall men 5 a few new pens
6 These volleyballs

Grammar Test ▸▸Unit 5~6

1 It's small 2 It's expensive 3 It's dirty
4 It's cold 5 cute socks 6 a few 7 long
8 many[a lot of] 9 O 10 many tall
11 little 12 many 13 few 14 a few
15 little 16 a little 17 much
18 This is an interesting book.
19 They're famous lawyers.
20 a fun magazine 21 this delicious yogurt

22 little money 23 a new camera
24 a few warm blankets
25 a few cups of hot water
26 ② 27 ④ 28 ① 29 ①, ③ 30 ②, ④ 31 ②, ④
32 ①, ④

UNIT 07 who, what

A 1 Whose 2 Who 3 What
4 Who[Whom] 5 What 6 Who

B 1 ⓐ 2 ⓓ 3 ⓑ 4 ⓒ

C 1 Who is your science teacher?
2 Who[Whom] are you looking at?
3 Whose book is this?
4 What are you listening to?
5 Who is making pasta?

D 1 Who opened the window last night?
2 Whose bags are those?
3 What are you reading?
4 Who was your classmate?
5 What animal do you like most?

UNIT 08 where, when, why

A 1 When 2 Why 3 Where 4 What
5 Where 6 Where 7 What 8 Why
9 When

B 1 ⓓ 2 ⓒ 3 ⓐ 4 ⓑ 5 ⓔ

C 1 is she 2 marry 3 are 4 do
5 does 6 go 7 is

UNIT 09 how

A 1 How long 2 How 3 How many
4 How far 5 How much 6 How often
7 How old 8 How much 9 How tall

B 1 many 2 is 3 O 4 is 5 many
6 is 7 are 8 did

C 1 How did you know that?
2 How much milk did you drink?
3 How many coins do you have?
4 How did you find the answer?
5 How many museums did she visit?
6 How much sugar do you need?

Grammar Test ▸▸Unit 7~9

1 How 2 Why 3 When
4 How 5 Where 6 Who
7 did you call 8 much 9 Who 10 is
11 When did he come back?
12 How much is it?
13 How long[much time] will it take?
14 Where is she?
15 How old are you?
16 What color do you like?
17 When[What time] did you get up?
18 ⓑ 19 ⓒ 20 ⓐ
21 When will you graduate?
22 Who[Whom] are you talking to?
23 How did you meet her?
24 How often do you update your computer?
25 When did you buy your cell phone?
26 Where did you download the song?

27 Who took this picture?

28 ③ 29 ①, ③ 30 ①, ④ 31 ④ 32 ①

UNIT 10 비인칭 주어 it

A 1 It is sunny today. 2 O

3 It is summer in Korea. 4 O

5 It is four fifteen.

B 1 date, It's 2 day, it, It's 3 It's 4 it's

C 1 it 2 It 3 It is 4 It 5 It is

D 1 It is cold today.

2 It rained all day long.

3 It is 5 o'clock in the morning.

4 It's 40 miles from here to the national park.

Grammar Test ▸▸Unit 10

1 What time is it 2 How far is it 3 How is

4 What day is it 5 What is the date

6 What season 7 It is 8 What day is it 9 it

10 It is 11 What 12 It 13 ② 14 ① 15 ③, ④

MEMO

MEMO

MEMO

MEMO

GRAMMAR BEAN

그래머빈 With Workbook

Beginning! 영어 초보자들을 배려한 쉽고 간결한 문법 설명
Easy! 쉽고 재미있는 다양한 연습 문제 수록
Active! 문법 학습을 통한 자신 있는 영어 쓰기
New! 예비중 새내기를 위한 중등 내신 대비용 문항 확충